TORAH

The Growing Gift

Steven E. Steinbock

Illustrated by Timothy Granger Smith

UAHC Press
New York, New York

Library of Congress Cataloging-in-Publication Data

Steinbock, Steven E.
    Torah: the growing gift/by Steven E. Steinbock; illustrated by Timothy Granger Smith.
        p. cm.
    Includes bibliographical references (p.   )
    ISBN 0-8074-0502-7: $8.00
    1. Bible. O.T. Pentateuch—Textbooks.   2. Jewish religious education—Textbooks for children.
[1. Bible. O.T. Pentateuch.]   I. Smith, Timothy Granger, ill. II. Bible. O.T. Pentateuch.
English. Selections. 1994. III. Title.
BS1227.S73 1994
222'.1061—dc20

Designed by Carla Weise/Levavi & Levavi

94-283
CIP
AC

20   19   18   17   16   15   14   13   12   11

Contents

Acknowledgments

While writing *Torah: The Growing Gift,* I came to appreciate anew that *talmud* Torah is a lifelong endeavor. I have grown with this book. The process of writing it has cultivated my own understanding of Torah and of young people.

Deep thanks to my editor, David P. Kasakove, for his patient guidance throughout this project, from germination to harvest. Thanks also to those who read all or part of the manuscript and offered valuable advice: Rabbi Howard I. Bogot, Robin Eisenberg, Aron Hirt-Manheimer, Judith G. Lichtig, Rabbi Bernard H. Mehlman, Connie R. Reiter, Dr. Lenore Sandel, Rabbi Daniel B. Syme, and Rabbi Bernard M. Zlotowitz. I also extend my thanks to Kathy Parnass for her fine copyediting, to Lori Stahl for her editorial assistance, and to Stuart L. Benick and Seymour Rossel for their careful guidance in helping to bring this book to fruition.

In addition, I was fortunate to have a number of junior editors who helped field-test my chapters. I am grateful to all of them, and especially to Stacey Rashti, the brightest fifth-grade scholar to shine her light on a writer's page. Their ideas, advice, and feedback are greatly appreciated.

For their encouragement and support, I wish to thank my family—my wife, Sue; my mother, Jo Ann; and, of course, my own seedling, Nathaniel, who was born while I was completing this book.

Finally I wish to thank my teachers. In Jewish tradition we call a teacher *abba,* "father." I have been blessed with many wise and caring teachers. Not the least among them was my father, Richard Steinbock ז״ל. As a ceaseless storyteller, a patient listener, and a sower of seeds of creativity, he was the inspiration for this book. It is to his memory that I dedicate it.

God's Gift of Learning

This is a book about Torah תּוֹרָה. Torah is very important to the Jewish people. Like many other important things, Torah can be hard to understand. In this chapter you will begin to understand Torah by finding out what it is.

What is Torah? Here are some answers.

As you will see in the pages that follow, Torah is all these things . . . and much more.

A Book

The Torah is a book. Like many books the Torah is full of lessons and stories. Parents and teachers have read these stories to one another and to children for thousands of years. Originally the Torah was written in Hebrew.

In some books you might read about Torah. In other books you might find a retelling of certain Torah stories. In this book you will read the Torah text itself.

A Scroll

The Torah is written on a scroll. A scroll is a long piece of parchment that is wound around two wooden strips.

There are no pages to turn in a scroll. You must wind the scroll to find the correct place.

A Torah written on a scroll is called a *Sefer Torah* סֵפֶר תּוֹרָה. Every letter in the *Sefer Torah* is written by a scribe, who is called a *sofer* סוֹפֵר. We keep a *Sefer Torah* inside the ark in the synagogue. We decorate the *Sefer Torah* with a cover, a breastplate, a crown, and a pointer, which is called a *yad* יָד.

Five Books

The Torah is made up of the Five Books of Moses. In Hebrew we call these books the *Chumash* חוּמָשׁ, which means "Five." The five books are:

1. Genesis. The Hebrew title of this book is Bereshit בְּרֵאשִׁית, which means "When [God] Began."
2. Exodus. The Hebrew title of this book is Shemot שְׁמוֹת, which means "Names."
3. Leviticus. The Hebrew title of this book is Vayikra וַיִּקְרָא, "And [*Adonai*] Called."
4. Numbers. The Hebrew title of this book is Bemidbar בְּמִדְבַּר, which means "In the Desert."
5. Deuteronomy. The Hebrew title of this book is Devarim דְּבָרִים, which means "Words."

Jewish Teaching

The word *Torah* means "Teaching." Torah is a very special teacher. One way in which Torah teaches us is through *mitzvot* מִצְווֹת. *Mitzvot* are special Jewish responsibilities. The *mitzvot* listed in the Torah help us to lead good lives. The *mitzvot* also teach us how we can help make the world a better place. As you read this book, you will learn about many of these special teachings.

A Book of Stories

Sometimes the Torah teaches by telling stories. Some of the stories are sad. Some of the stories are happy.

We may not always like the way in which the stories turn out. We may not always agree with the way the people in the stories act or what they say.

As you read the Torah stories in this book, you will learn about people who had to make important decisions. You will also read about people who made mistakes. And you will learn about people who accomplished great things. In many ways the people you will meet in the Torah may remind you of yourself and those you know.

A Very Special Gift

According to Jewish tradition, God gave the Torah to Moses. God gave the Torah to the Jewish people as a gift of love. From Moses' time to today, Torah has been handed down from one generation to the next. Passing down the gift of Torah is also an expression of love.

When you study Torah and when you follow the teachings of Torah, you help to keep the gift of Torah alive. In this way you express your love for God and for the Jewish people.

A Tree of Life

You may know the song "Tree of Life עֵץ חַיִּים." It is sung in the synagogue. The Torah is a Tree of Life. How is the Torah like a tree? Does the Torah have branches? Or leaves? Or roots?

Look at the illustration. In the blank spaces write the part of the Torah that is most like each part of a tree. Choose words from the Word List below or come up with your own.

WORD LIST

Stories	Lessons
Books	Crown
Ideas	Parchment
Chapters	*Mitzvot*
Words	Letters
Yad	Breastplate

Summary

In this chapter you learned that Torah is many things. It is a book made up of five books. The words of Torah can be printed in a book or written on a scroll. Torah is filled with *mitzvot*, stories, and other teachings. It is a special gift and a Tree of Life.

You will begin to read selections from the Torah—called Torah texts—in the next chapter. As you read from the Torah, you will discover how it is possible for one book to be so many things at the same time.

CHAPTER ONE

The Story of Creation

In this chapter you will begin to read from the first book of the Torah, the Book of Genesis. The Hebrew title of this book is Bereshit בְּרֵאשִׁית. Genesis is about beginnings. The first stories you will read tell of the Creation of the world. These stories explore some of life's great mysteries.

⊡⊡⊡⊡⊡⊡⊡⊡⊡⊡⊡⊡⊡⊡⊡⊡⊡⊡⊡⊡⊡⊡⊡⊡⊡⊡⊡⊡⊡

The Creation of Heaven and Earth

*T*he Torah begins with the story of Creation. This story tells how God created the world and everything in it. God made something new every day for six days.

As you read this story, ask yourself why Creation is spread out over six different days. If God can make and do anything, why do you think that it took God six days to create the world?

When God began to create the heaven and the earth, the world was empty and had no shape. Everything was dark.

God said, "Let there be light." And there was light. And God saw that the light was good. God separated light from dark. God called the light Day and the darkness Night. There was evening and there was morning, a **first day**.

God said, "Let the air be separated from the water." And it was so. God called the separation Sky. There was evening and there was morning, a **second day**.

God said, "Let the water below the sky be gathered into one area so that the dry land may appear." And it was so. God called the dry land Earth and the waters Sea. And God saw that it was good.

God said, "Let the earth sprout vegetation—plants and fruit trees of every kind." And it was so. And God saw that

it was good. There was evening and there was morning, a **third day**.

God said, "Let there be lights in the sky to separate day from night—to show the times and to shine on the earth." And it was so. God made the sun to shine during the day and the moon and stars to shine at night. And God saw that it was good. There was evening and there was morning, a **fourth day**.

God said, "Let the waters bring forth living creatures and birds that fly across the sky." And God created all the animals that swim and fly. And God saw that it was good. God blessed them, saying, "Be fertile and multiply." There was evening and there was morning, a **fifth day**.

God said, "Let the earth bring forth every kind of living creature—cattle, creeping things, and wild beasts of every kind." And it was so. God made every kind of animal. And God saw that it was good. God said, "Let us make Adam to be responsible for the earth." And God made Adam in the image of God, male and female God created them. God blessed them and said, "Be fertile and multiply. You are responsible for the earth and all the creatures on it. I give you every plant and tree to use for food. And to all the animals on the land, to all the birds of the sky, and to everything that creeps on the earth, I give all the green plants for food." And it was so. And God saw everything that God had made and found that it was very good. There was evening and there was morning, a **sixth day**.

The heaven and the earth were finished. On the **seventh day**, God stopped creating. God blessed the seventh day and made it holy because on it God rested from all the work of Creation.

The Order of Creation

Read the Torah text again. Something new was created on each day. Below is a chart listing the six days of Creation and Shabbat. Under the chart is a Word List of the things that God created. On lines **A**, **B**, and **C**, write the names of the items that appear on the Word List under the day on which they were created.

WORD LIST

Land animals	Light	Earth	Birds
Rest	Sky	People	Stars
Sea	Moon	Trees	Fish
Sun			

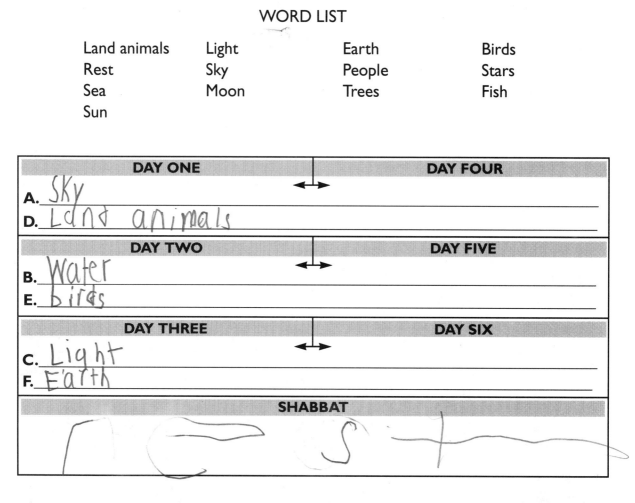

DAY ONE	DAY FOUR
A. _Sky_	
D. _Land animals_	
DAY TWO	**DAY FIVE**
B. _Water_	
E. _birds_	
DAY THREE	**DAY SIX**
C. _Light_	
F. _Earth_	
SHABBAT	

Look at the days that are listed next to each other on the chart. Can you find a relationship between the things that were created on those days? On lines **D**, **E**, and **F**, identify the patterns in the seven days of Creation.

Bonus Question: To find another pattern, look at the Torah text and count how often you find the word *good*. ☐

Write your answer in the box. ☐

In the Image of God

Find the place in the Torah text that states, "And God made Adam in the image of God, male and female God created them." In this story all people are called *Adam* אָדָם.

The Jewish people believe that God is invisible. But if God is invisible, what does the Torah mean when it says that God made male and female in the image of God?

In what ways are you made in the image of God? Below are two incomplete sentences. In the space provided complete each statement.

I am made in the image of God when I	I see the image of God in other people when I

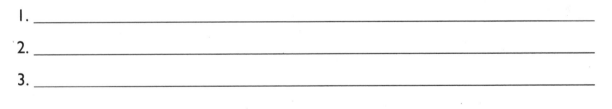

The Seventh Day

When Jews observe Shabbat, we remember God's Creation. Based on the Torah text, can you think of three different ways in which you can celebrate God's Creation on Shabbat?

1. _____

2. _____

3. _____

Summary

In the story of the seven days of Creation, you learned many important truths about people and the world. You learned that the world is a good place and that it was created in an organized way. You read that because people are created in God's image, they are able to create, organize, love, and rest. You discovered that we observe Shabbat, the final step of Creation, each week because it reminds us of the blessings of Creation and of rest.

CHAPTER TWO

Adam and Eve

In Chapter 1 you read a Torah text about God's Creation of the world. You learned that the world is good and that all people are created in God's image. In this chapter you will read another Creation story from Genesis. This one, however, tells about the difficulties of being human. You will meet Adam and Eve and their children, Cain and Abel.

◻◻◻◻◻◻◻◻◻◻◻◻◻◻◻◻◻◻◻◻◻◻◻◻◻◻◻◻◻◻◻◻

The Garden of Eden

This second story of Creation comes right after the first one in the Torah. God made Adam from the dust of the earth and blew the breath of life into his nose. Adam became a living being.

God planted a garden in Eden and put Adam in it. God planted many beautiful and nourishing trees. The Tree of Life was in the middle of the garden, as well as the Tree of Knowledge of Good and Bad.

God took Adam and placed him in the Garden of Eden to till it and tend it. God commanded Adam, saying, "You may eat from every tree in the garden except the Tree of Knowledge of Good and Bad. If you eat from it, you shall die."

God said, "It is not good for man to be alone. Adam should have a partner." And so God made every kind of animal and bird and brought them to Adam to name them. And Adam gave names to all the animals. But for Adam, no fitting partner was found.

So God cast a deep sleep upon Adam. While Adam slept, God took one of his ribs and made the rib into a woman. And God brought her to the man.

Then Adam said, "This one at last is bone of my bones and flesh of my flesh. She shall be called woman because she was taken from man." The two of them, the man and his wife, were naked, but they felt no shame.

Now the snake was the most sneaky animal that God had made. He said to the woman, "Did God really tell you not to eat from any of the trees in the garden?"

The woman answered, "We may eat the fruit of any of the trees except that of the tree in the middle of the garden. God told us that if we eat from it or even touch it, we will die."

The snake said to the woman, "You will not die if you eat from the tree in the middle of the garden. If you eat from that tree, your eyes will open and you will know the difference between good and bad, just like God."

The woman saw that the tree was pretty, good for eating, and full of wisdom. She took from its fruit and ate it. She also gave some to her husband, and he ate.

Then their eyes were opened, and they saw that they were naked. And they sewed together fig leaves and made clothing. They heard the sound of God moving about in the wind. The

God said to the woman, "What have you done?"

The woman replied, "The snake tricked me, and I ate."

Then God said to the snake, "Because of what you did, you will crawl on your belly, and women and their children will hate you."

God said to the woman, "In pain shall you bear children."

To Adam God said, "From now on, you must work hard for your food. By the sweat of your brow you shall get bread to eat until you return to the ground, because from it you were taken. Dust you are, and to dust you shall return."

man and his wife hid from God among the trees of the garden.

God called out, "Where are you?"

Adam replied, "When I heard You, I was afraid because I was naked, so I hid in the trees."

God said, "How did you know that you were naked? Did you eat from the tree that I had told you not to eat from?"

Adam said, "The woman you put at my side—she gave me fruit from the tree, and I ate."

The man named his wife Eve because she was the mother of all life. God made garments of skins for Adam and Eve and clothed them.

God said, "People are now like Me, knowing good and bad. What if they also eat from the Tree of Life and live forever?"

So God sent Adam and Eve out of the Garden of Eden and made Adam till the soil.

GENESIS 2:7-9, 2:15-3:23

Stories and Symbols

A symbol is a word or a picture that stands for or reminds us of something else.

On the left is one kind of symbol. People use flags as a symbol of the country, state, or province in which they live.

This flag has nothing on it. What does your country's flag look like? Draw the symbols that appear on your country's flag on this flag.

Do you know the meaning of the symbols on your country's flag? What do you think about when you see your country's flag? Write your answer below.

_____

_____

_____

_____

The symbol on the right is a six-pointed star known as the Magen David, "Shield of David." Today this symbol is found in the center of the Israeli flag and appears in synagogues throughout the world. Many Jews wear this symbol around their neck. Can you suggest why?

_____

_____

_____

_____

Look at the illustrations below. Complete the sentence under each picture, based on what the symbol is telling us.

The person is

_____.

The person is

_____.

The person is

_____.

The flame on the right can also be a symbol. List as many meanings as you can for this symbol.

_____

_____

_____

_____

_____

_____

In the story you just read, God planted two trees in the garden. One tree was the Tree of Life. The other tree was the Tree of Knowledge of Good and Bad.

The Tree of Life and the Tree of Knowledge of Good and Bad may not have been real trees. The Garden of Eden might not have been a real place. Both may be symbols that are meant to teach us important lessons.

In Chapter 1 you learned that the Tree of Life may be a symbol for the Torah. What else can a tree symbolize? List as many possibilities as you can.

_____

_____

_____

Read the Torah text again. Be sure to note carefully what is said about the trees in the garden. Why did Adam and Eve eat the fruit from the Tree of Knowledge of Good and Bad? How were Adam and Eve changed after they ate the fruit? Why did God force them out of the garden?

Use the spaces below to explain what you think each of the following symbols represents.

Garden of Eden

Tree of Life

Tree of Knowledge of Good and Bad

Knowing Right from Wrong

Both Adam and Eve did things that were wrong.
List the things they did that they were not supposed to do.

What Adam Did Wrong:	What Eve Did Wrong:

Do you think Adam and Eve knew that what they were doing was wrong? Circle your answer. **YES   NO**   Explain your answer.

_____

How do you know when *you* have done something wrong?

_____

Why do you think that Adam and Eve tried to hide when God called out to them?

_____

Have you ever wanted to hide after you did something wrong?

_____

The knowledge of right and wrong is called morality or ethics. Sometimes it is hard to know right from wrong. Doing the right thing is like climbing a tree that is very tall. The Torah, our Tree of Life, makes our climb easier and safer. It teaches us many lessons about right and wrong. It shows us how to behave so that we can help other people and make the world a better place.

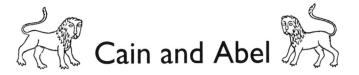

Cain and Abel

After Adam and Eve left the Garden of Eden, Eve gave birth to two boys, Cain and Abel. The brothers did not get along. In this Torah text you will read about a terrible tragedy. This story teaches us about the value of human life.

Abel became a keeper of sheep, and Cain became a tiller of the soil. Cain brought an offering to *Adonai* from the fruit of the soil, and Abel brought an offering from the finest of his flock. *Adonai* noticed Abel and his offering. But *Adonai* did not notice Cain's offering. Cain was very upset.

Adonai said to Cain, "Why are you upset? Why is your face fallen? Surely, if you do right, you will be raised up. But if you do not do right, then sin will get the best of you. Yet you can master the evil urge."

Cain said some words to his brother, Abel. And when they were in the field, Cain rose up against his brother and killed him. *Adonai* said to Cain, "Where is your brother, Abel?"

And Cain replied, "I do not know. Am I my brother's keeper?"

Then God said, "What have you done? Listen, your brother's blood cries out to Me from the ground."

Cain had to leave the presence of *Adonai*. He settled in the land of Nod, east of Eden.

GENESIS 4:1-16

The First Murder

Cain committed the world's first murder. Answer the following questions about this terrible crime.

Why do you think that God favored Abel's offering over Cain's? Circle the answer that you think is correct.

a. God did not like fruit.

b. Cain's offering was smaller than Abel's.

c. Abel's offering was from the finest of his flock, while Cain's offering consisted of ordinary fruit.

d. God favored Abel because he was better looking than Cain.

The Torah does not tell us what Cain said to his brother. Create your own dialogue between Cain and Abel.

Cain: _____

Abel: _____

Cain: _____

Abel: _____

Summary

In this chapter you learned that the Torah uses many symbols to teach its lessons. You discovered several symbols in the story of the Garden of Eden.

You also learned that the knowledge of right and wrong is called morality or ethics. Torah teaches us many lessons about right and wrong.

Noah and the Flood

God created the world. But the Torah tells us that the world wasn't exactly the way God had hoped it would be. People acted wickedly toward one another. The earth was filled with violence.

In this chapter you will read that God nearly destroyed the world with a great flood. You will learn that God made a special agreement, called a covenant, with Noah and his descendants. This covenant gave new hope for the future of God's Creation.

□ □

The Flood

The story of the Flood is one of the most dramatic accounts in the entire Torah. As you read, try to answer these questions: Why did God decide to destroy the world? What agreement did God make with Noah after the Flood?

Adonai saw that people were acting in wicked ways. *Adonai* said, "I will destroy the people and the animals that I created. I regret that I made them."

But *Adonai* liked Noah. Noah was a righteous man. He was a good man in his time. Noah walked with God.

God said to Noah, "I am going to destroy all flesh because the earth is filled with violence and lawlessness on account of them. Make an ark out of gopher wood. I will bring a flood to destroy all living things. But I will make a covenant with you. Your family shall come into the ark, along with every type of animal."

Noah did everything that God commanded him. He took his family into the ark. Every animal came into the ark, two by two, male and female.

When the Flood came, it was as if the ocean had exploded and the sky had burst open. It rained for forty days and forty nights. The waters raised the ark above the earth so that it floated upon the waters. The rain continued until every hill and mountain of the earth was covered with water.

Every living being on the earth was destroyed. Only Noah and those who were with him in the ark lived. The waters continued for one hundred and fifty days.

God remembered Noah and all the animals in the ark. God sent a wind across the earth. The waters went down, and the ark came to rest on Mount Ararat.

Noah opened the window of the ark. He sent out a dove to see if the waters had dried up from the earth. But the dove found no place to land and returned to the ark.

After seven more days Noah again sent out the dove. This time the dove brought back an olive leaf. Then Noah knew that the waters had lowered from the earth.

After seven more days Noah again sent out the dove. This time it did not return to him anymore. Noah came out from the ark. He built an altar and made offerings to God.

God blessed Noah and his family and said, "Be fruitful and multiply. All the animals of the earth are given into your hand. You shall be responsible for them. You may eat the meat of the animals, but you may not eat the animals live or eat their blood. You shall also be responsible for other people. You must not kill any person. All people are created in God's image.

"I make My covenant with you, all your children, and all living beings that I will never again destroy the earth with a flood. I have put My rainbow in the clouds. It is a sign and a reminder of the covenant between Me and all people and animals that live on the earth."

GENESIS 6:5-8:12, 20; 9:1-17

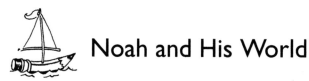

Noah and His World

It is hard to imagine a world so bad that God would want to destroy it. But if people were behaving as badly as the Torah says, their violence would have destroyed the world if God had not brought on the Flood.

Can you imagine a world that has been destroyed by violence? Science-fiction literature is full of stories about worlds that are destroyed by wars, bombs, and pollution. Worlds destroyed in these ways might never be able to heal themselves.

In this Torah text the Flood destroyed all living beings except those that were in the ark. But life can return to a world destroyed by a flood. By cleansing the world with a flood, God gave the world a second chance.

Imagine that you are Noah. God has just told you of the plan to bring on the great Flood. Write down your response to God's idea.

NO it is a bad idea because where will we live?

God didn't let Noah or his family drown in the Flood. Why do you think that God decided to save Noah?

He saved Noah because Noah maybe was nice to g-d.

What do you think the Torah means when it says that Noah "walked with God"?

He did what g-d said for him to do to survive

Think about a time when you felt as if you were walking with God. What made you feel that way? What was it like? Describe that feeling in the space below.

I felt kinta wiert,

The Torah text says that Noah was a "righteous man." The Hebrew word for a righteous person is *tzadik* צַדִּיק. The word *tzadik* means "one who acts right." We don't use this word very often. We only use the word to describe a very special person.

Why do you think that Noah was called a *tzadik*?

He saved animals and humans

The Rainbow

A covenant is a promise. The Hebrew word for covenant is *brit* בְּרִית. The *brit* in this story is a promise not only between God and Noah but between God and all living creatures. God has promised that the world will never again be destroyed by a flood. The symbol of this *brit* is the rainbow.

Every *brit* works two ways. God has made a promise to us. In return, God asks us to promise to obey certain rules. The Torah teaches us that rules not only protect the world, they can also help us become better people. The Torah gives us rules to live by. We call these rules *mitzvot*. Read the Torah text again and list the *mitzvot* that God gave to Noah.

1. *G-d destroyed*
2. *rain continued to fall the earth with a flood 150*
3. *Noah dit anything got commanded him. day and nights*
4. *Take care your pets*
5. *Be fruitful ant multiply*
6. *eat the meat only of dead animals*

During Noah's time God's Creation was being spoiled by the cruel and careless behavior of people. The symbol of the rainbow reminds us of our promise to be good, to behave righteously, and to walk with God.

The earth today is in danger of being destroyed by pollution. The rainbow reminds us of God's promise never again to destroy the earth with a flood. The rainbow also reminds us of our promise to take care of the earth and our environment.

In the space below use a rainbow to design a poster advertising our covenant with God to behave righteously and to take care of God's Creation.

Summary

In this chapter you read that because God was disappointed with people's behavior, God brought on a flood to destroy the living creatures on the earth. God chose one man, Noah, to lead a new generation of Creation. God made a *brit* with Noah and all his descendants. God promised that the world would never again be destroyed by a flood. Noah accepted God's *mitzvot*. Today the rainbow is a symbol and a reminder to us of our *brit* to behave responsibly by treating one another fairly and taking care of our environment.

Abraham's New Direction

Change can be frightening. In Chapter 3 you read about a flood that changed the face of Creation. After the Flood, God and Noah entered into a covenant. This covenant changed the future of humanity.

In this chapter you will learn about Abraham, a man of many changes. Abraham showed how important it is to try out new ideas. You will learn that a new religion was born when God made a covenant with Abraham and his family.

◻◻◻◻◻◻◻◻◻◻◻◻◻◻◻◻◻◻◻◻◻◻◻◻◻◻◻◻◻◻◻◻◻

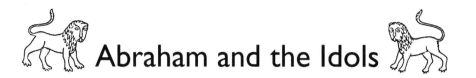

Abraham and the Idols

*T*he following story is a midrash מִדְרָשׁ. A midrash *is a story that is based on the contents of the Torah.*

For most of his life, Abraham had another name. His name was Abram אַבְרָם.

As a child, Abram used to work in his father's shop. Abram's father made idols for a living. Abram would watch his father make statues of gods.

One day Abram's father left the shop to deliver some idols to a customer.

Abram looked at all the idols. Some were shaped like birds and others like bulls. Some looked like lions and others like people. Some were supposed to guarantee to make you rich, and others would help your fields produce many crops. One kind of idol was supposed to make you beautiful, while another would help you have many children.

Suddenly Abram realized a very important idea. Abram's idea seems obvious to us today, but it was a new idea to the people of Abram's time. The boy understood that clay statues cannot be gods. There is only one God. Abram knew that God didn't look like a bird or a lion or even a person. He knew that people couldn't see or touch God, the way they could see and touch statues. And they certainly couldn't own God.

So Abram picked up a big stick and smashed all the idols in his father's shop.

When his father returned, the shop was in shambles. Clay dust was everywhere. In the middle of the shop, one large idol was still standing. In the idol's hand was the stick that Abram had used to destroy the other idols. Abram's father asked him what had happened.

Abram replied, "The idols began to argue about which one was the strongest. This big one smashed all the little idols. He is the winner."

His father was very angry and said, "It's just a statue that I made with my own hands. It couldn't have smashed anything."

"Yes, Father," said little Abram. "Then why do people worship idols?"

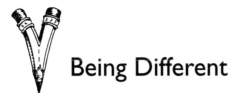

Being Different

Young Abraham was very brave. He thought ideas that other people were too afraid to think. He said words that others were too frightened to say. He was a person who thought for himself.

Abraham stood up for what he believed in. He did what he knew was the right thing. Sometimes standing up for your beliefs and doing the right thing is frightening.

Have you ever felt that the people around you—your friends or classmates, brothers or sisters—were doing something wrong? Sometimes we think differently or believe in God differently or celebrate different holidays than other people do.

In the space below tell about a time when you felt that you were different from those around you.

How did it feel to be different?

_____

_____

_____

_____

The Family of Abraham

Have you ever made a family tree? A family tree is a special kind of chart. Family trees show how people are related to one another. Below is a family tree. Fill in the names in the boxes. Do you have brothers or sisters? Where would you put them on your chart? Make a box on your tree for each of your brothers and sisters.

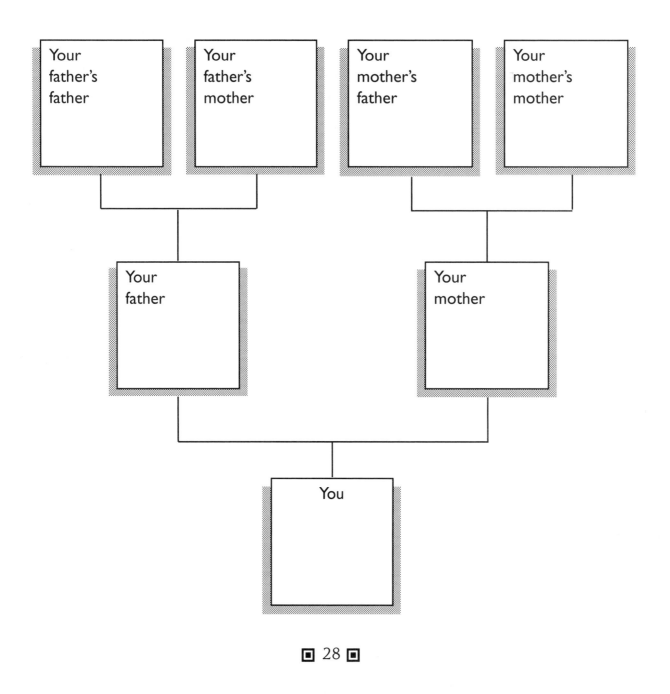

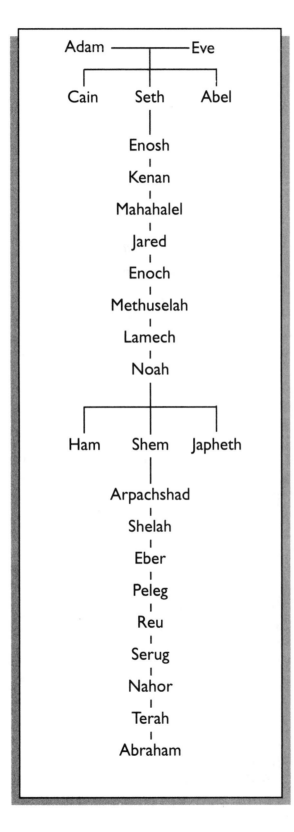

This family tree shows how Adam and Eve, Noah, and Abraham are all part of the same family. They are separated by many generations.

One level on a family tree is called a generation. Adam and Eve are part of one generation. Cain, Seth, and Abel are part of the next generation. Each level on the chart is a generation. How many generations can you count on this chart?

Abraham is a descendant of Noah. *Descendant* is a word for children, grandchildren, and great-grandchildren. If you have children, they, their children, and all the children who come after them will be your descendants.

Find Noah's name in the middle of the chart. Noah's three children are named Ham, Shem, and Japheth.

Shem's son is named _____.

Shem's grandson is named _____.

Nahor's son is named_____.

Terah's son is named_____.

Go Forth

Hebrew is a language. Hebrew is also a word that means "Jew." Abraham was the first Hebrew.

The word Hebrew *comes from the word* Ivri עִבְרִי*, which means "to cross over." Abraham crossed over in many ways. He crossed over by challenging the worship of many gods. He crossed over by being different. In this Torah text you will read about how Abraham crossed over to a new land.*

Adonai said to Abram, "Go forth from your native land and from your father's house. Go to the land that I will show you. I will make of you a great nation. I will bless you. I will make your name great, and you shall be a blessing. I will bless those who bless you and curse those who curse you. All the families of the earth shall bless themselves by you."

Abram went forth as *Adonai* had commanded him. He took his wife Sarai and his orphaned nephew Lot and all the wealth they owned.

When they arrived in the land of Canaan, God appeared to Abram and said, "I will give this land to your descendants."

GENESIS 12:1-7

Finding New Directions

Can you think of a time when you had to go to a new place? Write down the name of the place in the space below.

Yankee Stadium   bathroom

Try to remember what going to this new place felt like. Write down your feelings in the space below.

it had a white seat

Going to new places can be scary. But good things can happen when people go to new places. What are some of the good things that happened when you went to your new place?

the white seat had a leather that you pull down that makes a noise

Why do you think that Abraham obeyed God's command to go to a new land?

because god didn't want abraham to die in the floor

In this Torah text God made a *brit* with Abraham. Put a check [✔] next to the promises that God made to Abraham.

_____ large family   _____ power

_____ blessings   _____ land to Abraham's descendants

_____ wealth   _____ leadership of an important nation

What does God ask Abraham to promise in return? Why does God ask this?

_____

_____

The Father of Many Nations

*D*id you ever wonder why Abram's name was changed to Abraham? Names *are very important in the Torah. Names are also important to us today. Our names are part of what we are.*

Read the following Torah text, which tells how Abraham got his name and how his brit *with God grew.*

When Abram was ninety-nine years old, *Adonai* appeared to him and said, "I am *El Shaddai*. Walk in My ways and be good. I will establish My covenant between you and Me and give you many descendants. This is My covenant with you: I will make you the father of many nations. Your name shall be changed from Abram to Abraham. I will make you fertile and make many nations of you. And kings will be your descendants. I will keep My covenant with you and your descendants forever. I will give this land in which you live, all the land of Canaan, to you and your descendants as an everlasting possession. I will be their God."

God then said to Abraham, "You and all your descendants shall keep My covenant throughout the ages. Every male among you shall be circumcised as a sign of the covenant between Me and you. And throughout the generations, every male among you shall be circumcised when he is eight days old.

"As for your wife Sarai, you shall not call her Sarai, but her name shall be Sarah. I will bless her and she will have a son."

Abraham threw himself on his face and laughed as he said to himself, "How can we have children? I am nearly one hundred years old, and Sarah is ninety."

God said, "Nevertheless, Sarah will give birth to a son, and you shall name him Isaac. And I will keep My covenant with him and his descendants to come."

GENESIS 17:1-19

The Covenant

In this Torah text God tells Abraham to have all the male members of his community circumcised as a sign of the *brit* between God and Abraham. In Hebrew this ceremony is called *Brit Milah* בְּרִית מִילָה.

For Jews, *Brit Milah* is a special ceremony. According to the Torah text, how old is a baby when the *Brit Milah* is performed?

Brit Milah is a very happy event for the entire family. It is a time that the baby's parents share with relatives and friends. Special prayers are said, and food is served. *Brit Milah* can take place in a home, a hospital, or a synagogue.

It is a special *mitzvah* to celebrate the birth of a daughter with a ceremony called *Brit Chayim* בְּרִית חַיִּים.

Brit Chayim can take place either in a home or a synagogue when a baby girl is eight days old. During the *Brit Chayim* ceremony, holiday candles are lit and special prayers are said by the baby's parents and a rabbi.

Summary

You read in this chapter about Abraham, the first Hebrew. Abraham had the courage to believe in one God even though the people around him believed in many gods. Through *Adonai*'s covenant with Abraham, people all over the world changed the way they understood God. This covenant, or *brit*, led to the birth of the Jewish people.

The story of Abraham reminds us that we should stand up for our beliefs, even if we sometimes must stand alone.

The Testing Of Abraham

The stories in the Torah describe God in many different ways. In the Garden of Eden, Adam and Eve heard the sound of God moving about in the wind. In the story of the Flood, Noah heard God's voice. Sometimes God's presence appeared in a dream. In this chapter you will read about two of the times that God appeared to Abraham. On each of these occasions, God tested Abrahams loving-kindness. In the second story God tested Abraham's faith.

◨ ◨

Revelation

Revelation means "something that is seen." A person who has seen or heard God is said to have had a revelation.

The following story is about a revelation. It begins with the words "God appeared." But when Abraham looked up, he saw three men coming toward him. Tradition teaches that these men were angels. As you read the Torah text, try to think of your own explanation for how God appeared to Abraham.

God appeared to Abraham while he was sitting at the entrance of his tent as the day grew hot. Abraham looked up and saw three men walking toward him.

He ran out to greet them and said, "My lords, please stop and rest with me. Let me bring you some water. Bathe your feet. I will bring you some bread." Abraham ran into the tent to Sarah and they prepared cakes, tender veal, cheese, and milk. Abraham put these foods before the visitors and waited on them under the tree as they ate.

They said to him, "Where is your wife Sarah?"

He replied, "She is in the tent."

Then one of them said, "Sarah shall have a son."

Sarah was listening at the entrance of the tent, and she laughed to herself, saying, "Shall I bear a son at my age?"

Then God said to Abraham, "Why did Sarah laugh? Nothing is too wonderful for God to do. I will return to you when the time is right, and Sarah shall have a son."

GENESIS 18:1-14

How Do We "See" God?

At the beginning of this chapter, you learned that a revelation is an experience of seeing God. Explain how you think God was revealed to Abraham.

_____

_____

_____

Some people think that God "appears" through acts of loving-kindness, *gemilut chasadim* גְּמִילוּת חֲסָדִים. Read the story again. How many kind acts performed by Abraham for the visitors can you find? Make a list of the acts in the box below.

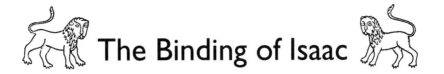

The Binding of Isaac

After the visit by the three men, God's promise of giving Abraham and Sarah a child came true. The couple had a son, whom they named Isaac. They loved Isaac very much. The text you will read is called the Akeda עֲקֵדָה, which means "Binding," because it tells how Isaac was bound on the altar at Mount Moriah.

God tested Abraham. God said to him, "Abraham."

Abraham answered, "Here I am."

God said, "Take your son, your favorite one, Isaac, whom you love. Go to the land of Moriah. Offer him as a burnt offering on a hill that I will show you."

Early the next morning Abraham packed his donkey. He took his two servants, his son Isaac, and some wood for the burnt offering, and he set out for the place that God had told him about. On the third day Abraham looked up and saw the place from far away.

Then Abraham said to his servants, "You stay here with the donkey. The boy and I will go and worship, and then we'll return."

Abraham gave the firewood to his son Isaac to carry. Abraham took the firestone and the knife, and the two walked off together. Then Isaac said to his father, "I see the firestone and the wood. But where is the sheep for the burnt offering?"

Abraham said, "God will see to the sheep, my son." And they walked on together.

When they arrived at the place that God had told him about, Abraham built an altar. He laid out the wood and bound his son Isaac. Abraham put Isaac on the altar, on top of the wood. And Abraham picked up the knife to slay his son.

Then an angel of *Adonai* called to him from heaven, "Abraham! Abraham!"

And he answered, "Here I am."

And God said, "Do not raise your hand against the boy or do anything to him. For now I know that you fear God. You would even give your favorite son to Me."

When Abraham looked up, he saw a ram caught in a bush by its horns. He offered the ram as an offering instead of his son. Abraham called the place Adonai Yireh, as it is said, "On the mountain of God there is vision."

GENESIS 22:1-14

The Revelation of the Akeda

1. Explain how God tested Abraham.

_____

_____

2. Abraham's revelation in this Torah text is quite different from his revelation in the story of the three men. How does God appear to Abraham in the *Akeda* story?

_____

_____

3. What do you think that Abraham learned from his revelation in the *Akeda* story?

_____

_____

_____

4. The Torah does not tell us what Isaac was thinking. In the space below write what you think might have been going through Isaac's mind.

_____

_____

_____

Summary

In this chapter you learned that *revelation* is the term that is used to describe a time when a person sees or hears God. Abraham saw God in several ways. You read Torah texts telling about two of Abraham's revelations. First three men, or angels, announced that Sarah would bear a child. Then God tested Abraham's faith by commanding Abraham to sacrifice that child, Isaac. In the next chapter you will learn more about Abraham's family.

From Generation to Generation

Abraham faced many changes in his life. People face many changes as they grow. Some changes are happy, like meeting new friends and celebrating important birthdays. Other changes, like losing friends and experiencing the death of loved ones, are sad.

In this chapter you will read about several changes that occurred in the family of Abraham and Sarah. Two people died and another person got married. As you read these stories, you will learn that change is an important part of family life.

☐ ☐

The Death of Sarah

Sarah, the wife of Abraham, died shortly after the *Akeda.* Some people think that Sarah died after she heard that Abraham had almost sacrificed Isaac. Whatever the cause of her death, Sarah was very old. According to Torah, she was one hundred and twenty-seven years old.

Abraham was very sad after Sarah's death. He spent some time—the Torah doesn't tell us how long—mourning. Mourning is a period of time in which people remember and show signs of sadness over the death of a loved one.

After mourning for Sarah, Abraham rose to perform a *mitzvah.* The Torah tells us that Abraham spoke to the Hittites, the people in whose country he was living. He said to them, "I am a stranger living among you. Sell me a burial site from your land so that I may bury my dead." (Genesis 23:4)

A Hittite named Ephron sold Abraham a piece of land in Machpelah. It included a field, a grove of trees, and a cave. Abraham buried his wife Sarah in the cave of Machpelah.

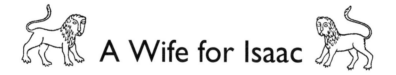

A Wife for Isaac

After Abraham buried Sarah, he took on another mitzvah. *You may be surprised by his next project.*

By now Abraham was old, advanced in years. *Adonai* had blessed him in many ways. Abraham said to one of his servants, "Go to the land of my birth and find a wife for my son Isaac."

The servant took ten of his master's camels and set out. He made his way to the city of Nahor. He made the camels kneel down by the well outside the city.

It was the time when the women came out to draw water.

He said, "Oh, *Adonai,* God of my master Abraham, give me good fortune today. Deal graciously with my master Abraham. Let the woman who offers water for my camels be the one whom You have chosen for Your servant Isaac."

He had hardly finished speaking

when a beautiful woman came out with a jar on her shoulder. It was Rebecca, the daughter of Bethuel, Abraham's relative.

The servant ran to her and said, "May I please have a sip of water from your jar?"

"Drink, my lord," she said, giving him water from her jar. "And let me get some water for your camels." She quickly filled the trough with water from her jar for the camels.

The servant stood gazing at her, silently wondering whether *Adonai* had made his mission successful. When the camels had finished drinking, the ser-

vant took a gold nose-ring and two gold bands for her arms. "Please tell me," he asked, "who are your parents? Is there room in your father's house for me to spend the night?"

She replied, "I am the daughter of Bethuel the son of Milcah. We have room for you to stay with us and plenty of straw for the camels."

The man bowed low to God and said, "Blessed is *Adonai* the God of Abraham, who has given steadfast kindness to my master Abraham and has guided me to the house of my master's relatives."

GENESIS 24:1-27

A Wife for Isaac: A Closer Look

In biblical times parents usually arranged the marriage of their children. Often people would marry cousins, distant relatives, or the son or daughter of family friends.

When Abraham's servant arrived in the city of Nachor, he prayed to God. Read over the part of the Torah text in which the servant prayed. What was he praying for?

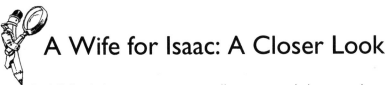

A wife for Issac, (his son).

The servant asked for a sign to help him recognize the right woman for Isaac. What was the sign?

It was rebacca the daughter of Bethuel a relative of abraham.

Why do you think the servant chose that sign to recognize Isaac's future bride?

She was a relative of adraham and the servent wanted issac to mary someone in his family.

People choose friends for different reasons. When you are trying to decide whom to choose as a friend, what "sign" do you look for?

The sign is someone who gets in trouble 1,000,000 times each year in school, not sunday school.

Some "action scenes" from the Torah text are described below.

Write a number from 1 to 8 in the box inside each of the boxes below to indicate the correct order of the scenes.

5	3	1	8
Rebecca offers water to the servant.	Rebecca comes to the well to draw water.	The servant takes ten camels and heads for Nahor.	The servant thanks God for finding a wife for Isaac.
2	7	6	4
The servant stops at a well and prays for help.	Rebecca offers to let the servant stay at her father's house.	Rebecca draws water for the servant's camels.	The servant asks Rebecca for a sip of water.

Look again at the description of the scenes above. Remember that the things people do show what kind of people they are. What kind of person was Rebecca? Explain your answer.

Rebeca is a helpful person because she gave water to the servent servents.

The Generation of Isaac

*T*his chapter has a happy ending. The servant took Rebecca back to Canaan with him. Read about the first meeting between Isaac and Rebecca.

Isaac went out walking in the field toward evening. Looking up, he saw camels approaching.

Rebecca raised her eyes and saw Isaac. She asked, "Who is that man walking toward us?"

The servant said, "That is Isaac, my master." The servant told Isaac about all the events of his journey.

Isaac took Rebecca as his wife. He loved her and found comfort after his mother's death.

*J*ust as this chapter began with a sad death, so, too, it ends with a death. We feel sad as we read about the passing of our ancestor Abraham, the first Hebrew.

Abraham lived to be one hundred and seventy-five years old. Abraham took his last breath and died at a ripe age, old and happy. His sons, Isaac and Ishmael, buried him in the field that he had bought from the Hittites. That is where Abraham is buried, together with his wife Sarah. After the death of Abraham, God blessed his son Isaac.

GENESIS 24:63-67, 25:7-11

Who Was Ishmael?

Ishmael was Isaac's older half brother. Ishmael's mother was Hagar, Sarah's maid. Abraham favored his second son, Isaac, and the Torah tells us little about his first son. Muslims believe that they, too, are descendants of Abraham through their ancestor Ishmael. While Isaac is the ancestor of the Jews, Ishmael is the ancestor of the Arabic people.

Summary

The Torah teaches that love and *mitzvot* are tied together like the knots of a bow. In this chapter you read about several changes that took place in the family of Abraham and Sarah. Abraham and his sons performed the *mitzvot* of burial and mourning. Abraham helped make it possible for Isaac to fulfill the *mitzvah* of marriage.

In the next chapter you will read about Isaac and Rebecca's performance of the *mitzvah* of creating a family.

CHAPTER SEVEN

Twins

In Chapter 6 you read about the marriage of Isaac and Rebecca. After Sarah's and Abraham's death, Isaac and Rebecca became the leaders of the next generation of the Hebrew people.

In this chapter you will read how Isaac and Rebecca raised a family of their own. You will also learn about the blessings that one generation gives the next.

■■■■■■■■■■■■■■■■■■■■■■■■■■■■■■■■■■

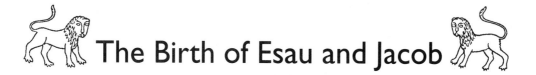

The Birth of Esau and Jacob

This is the story of Isaac, the son of Abraham. Isaac was forty years old when he married Rebecca. Isaac begged God for children because he and Rebecca did not have any. God responded, and Rebecca became pregnant.

But before they were born, the children struggled inside her. She said, "If this is so, why do I exist?"

God answered her, "Two nations are inside you. Two separate peoples will come out of your body. One will be stronger than the other. And the older shall serve the younger."

The time came for Rebecca to give birth. There were twins inside her. The first one that came out was red and hairy. They called him Esau.

His brother came out grabbing Esau's heel so they called him Jacob. Isaac was sixty years old when Esau and Jacob were born.

GENESIS 25:19-26

All in the Family

Why do you think that Isaac and Rebecca wanted children?

_____

_____

When Esau was about to be born, Jacob tried to pull him back. He grabbed his brother's heel because he wanted to be the older one. Why do you think that Jacob wanted to be the firstborn?

_____

_____

_____

Esau Sells His Birthright

When the boys grew up, Esau became a skillful hunter, a man of the outdoors. Jacob was a gentle man who stayed at home. Isaac liked Esau better because Esau brought him fresh game. But Rebecca preferred Jacob.

One day Jacob was cooking a stew. Esau came in from the field and said, "Give me some of that red stuff. I'm starving."

Jacob replied, "First sell me your birthright."

Esau said, "I'm starving to death so what good is my birthright to me?"

But Jacob said, "Promise me first."

So Esau promised his birthright to Jacob, and Jacob gave Esau bread and stew.

GENESIS 25:27-34

What Is a Birthright?

In ancient Canaan the oldest boy inherited twice as much property as all the other children when their father died. The right to inherit twice as much as the other children is called the birthright. Esau was entitled to the birthright because he was born first.

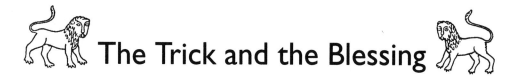

The Trick and the Blessing

Esau gave away his birthright. But he expected that his father would still give him a special blessing before Isaac died. In ancient times a blessing was especially important if it was given by a father to his children just before his death. People believed that such blessings were promises that would certainly come true.

In the following Torah text we see how Isaac was tricked into giving Jacob a special blessing.

When Isaac was old and his eyes were so dim that he could not see, he called Esau, his older son, and said, "My son."

And he answered, "Here I am."

And Isaac said, "I am old now. I don't know how soon I may die. Get your bow and arrows and go into the woods. Hunt me some game. Then cook it for me the way I like it. And I will give you my special blessing before I die."

Rebecca had been listening while Isaac was speaking to Esau. After Esau had gone out to hunt, Rebecca said to her son Jacob, "I heard your father ask your brother to bring him some game and prepare him a meal. Now listen carefully to my instructions. Go to the flock and get me the two best goats, and I will make your father's favorite meal. Then you will take it to your father so that he may bless you before he dies."

Jacob did what his mother told him. He brought in two goats from the flock, and Rebecca prepared a wonderful meal for Isaac. Then she put goat skins on Jacob's hands and neck to make Jacob feel more like Esau.

Jacob went to his father and said, "Father, it is I, Esau. I have done as you told me. Sit up and eat some of my meat, so that you may give me your special blessing."

Isaac said, "How did you finish so quickly, my son?"

And he answered, "God gave me good fortune."

Isaac said, "Come closer so that I may feel you."

So Jacob drew closer to Isaac. Isaac

felt him and wondered, "The voice is the voice of Jacob, but the hands are the hands of Esau." He asked, "Are you really my son Esau?"

Jacob answered, "I am."

Isaac then said, "Let me eat some of this meat so that I may give you my special blessing." Isaac ate and drank and then said to his son, "Come kiss me, my son."

And Jacob went and kissed him.

And Isaac smelled him and said, "Ah, the smell of my son is like the smell of God's blessed fields." And he blessed him with the words:

May God give you plenty of new
    grain and wine
from the dew of heaven and the fat
    of the earth.

May peoples serve you and nations
    bow down to you.
Be master over your brothers,
and let your mother's sons bow
    to you.
May those who curse you be cursed.
And may they who bless you be
    blessed.

GENESIS 27: 1-10, 18-29

When Esau found out that Jacob had stolen his blessing, he was very angry and decided to kill his brother. Rebecca thought that Jacob should go away for a while. She sent Jacob to live with her brother Laban in Haran.

Torah Detective

To better understand each of the people in this story, you're going to play a game. Imagine that you are a private detective. You've been hired to investigate Isaac's family. In order to prepare your evidence, fill out the forms below.

Name: **Isaac** Appearance?	Name: **Rebecca** Appearance?
In what ways is Isaac a good person?	Is Rebecca a good mother? A good wife? A good person?
What are Isaac's weaknesses?	Why does she do the things that she does?

Name: **Esau** Appearance?	Name: **Jacob** Appearance?
This man sold his birthright for a pot of stew. What does this tell you about his character?	Jacob's name means "heel." In English slang a heel is a selfish person, a scoundrel. In what way is Jacob a heel?
Esau does not hurt anyone. Then why do his mother and brother take advantage of him?	Is Jacob looking out for his own interest, or is he just following his mother's instructions?

Part of a detective's job is to determine a motive. A motive is the reason why a person acts. In each of the cases below, select the motive that seems the most accurate to you or write your own explanation in the space provided.

1. Isaac gave his blessing to Jacob because

    a. Isaac was too old and feeble to tell the difference between his sons.
    b. Isaac knew that Jacob was the more deserving son, and he only pretended to be fooled.

    c. _____

    _____

2. Rebecca helped Jacob steal the blessing because

    a. Rebecca never liked Esau and did not want to see him get anything.
    b. Rececca knew that Jacob would be a better leader of the Hebrew people.

    c. _____

    _____

3. Esau planned to kill Jacob because

    a. Esau felt that Jacob had taken advantage of him unfairly and deserved to be punished.
    b. Esau was not very smart, and, therefore, his only way to respond was to threaten Jacob with physical strength.

    c. _Jacob stool his blessing._

    _____

4. Jacob took his brother's birthright and blessing because

    a. Jacob was a greedy boy who grabbed everything that he could.
    b. Jacob was following his mother's instructions.

    c. _Esau was to much in command and rebbaca liked jacob more._

■ 51 ■

Write Your Own Blessing

The blessing that Isaac gave Jacob was very important. It was a promise of hope for Jacob's future.

Imagine that you are eighty years old. It is time to give a blessing to your oldest child. In the space below write a blessing for your child.

Blessing Checklist

May you be happy.

May you have many children.

May you learn many things.

May you have many friends.

May you be helpful to those around you.

May you be good like _____.

May you always think about others.

May you also think about yourself.

May you have plenty of food.

May you always study hard.

May you grow up to be a good person.

May you be protected by God's presence.

> My child,

Summary

In this chapter you learned that birthrights and blessings were important in the ancient world. You read how Jacob took advantage of his brother and tricked his father in order to receive Esau's birthright and blessing. In Chapters 8 and 9 you will follow Jacob as he begins to take responsibility for his actions.

Jacob Leaves Home

In Chapter 7 you read a Torah text in which Jacob tricked his father and stole his brother's blessing. In order to escape from his brother's rage, Jacob left home. On his journey Jacob had several experiences that helped him to grow up. You will read how God was revealed to Jacob in a strange dream and what Jacob did to start a family of his own in Haran.

⊡ ⊡

The Journey

Esau was very angry after Jacob tricked him of both his birthright and his blessing. He planned to kill Jacob. Jacob ran away to the city of Haran, where Rebecca's brother, Laban, lived.

The following text tells about the strange experience that Jacob had on his journey from Canaan.

Jacob left Beersheba and set out for Haran. He came to a certain place and stayed there for the night because the sun had set. He took one of the stones from that place and used it as a pillow.

He had a dream. A ladder was set on the ground. Its top reached to the sky. Angels of God were going up and down the ladder.

God was standing next to him and said: "I am *Adonai,* the God of your ancestor Abraham and the God of Isaac. I will give the ground on which you are lying to you and your descendants. They shall be as many as the dust of the earth. You shall spread out to the west and to the east, to the north and to the south. All the families of the earth shall bless themselves by you and your descendants. Remember that I am with you. I will protect you wherever you go, and I will bring you back to this land. I will not leave you until I have done all that I have promised you."

Jacob awoke from his sleep and said, *"Adonai* must be here in this place, and I didn't even know it." He shivered and said, "What an awesome place. God lives here. And this is the gateway to heaven."

Early in the morning Jacob took the stone that he had used as a pillow and poured oil on top of it. He named that place Bethel.

GENESIS 28:10-19

What Are Dreams?

The Torah text you have just read is unusual. It contains no action. Instead it describes a dream. Why do you think that the Torah tells us about a dream at this point in Jacob's life?

Can you remember a dream that you had last night? Even if you can't remember having had a dream, you probably had several. Doctors say that we spend more than one and a half hours dreaming each night. We have an average of four dreams during a single night's sleep. But most of us forget our dreams by the time we wake up.

Dreams can be made up of short scenes. The scenes in our dreams don't always make sense to us. We see and hear things in dreams that seem to be similar to things in real life, but they are different. Some dreams are fun. Some dreams are happy. But dreams can also be scary.

Draw a scene below from a dream that you once had.

Jacob's Ladder

The meaning of a dream is called an interpretation. Let's try to interpret Jacob's dream. One rule about interpreting dreams is that there is no right or wrong meaning to a dream.

To help you interpret Jacob's dream, recall what Jacob was thinking and doing before he had his dream. How do you think that Jacob felt that night? Was he happy? Sad? Scared? Angry?

You have learned about symbols in the Torah. A symbol can be a word, an image, or an event that stands for something else. Symbols help us to understand things in our lives.

In column **A** below list the symbols in Jacob's dream. In column **B** write the meaning of each symbol.

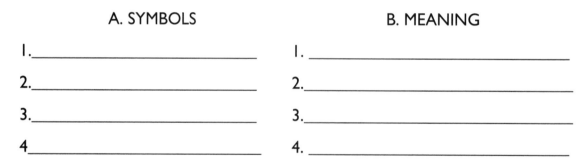

A. SYMBOLS

1._____

2._____

3._____

4._____

B. MEANING

1. _____

2. _____

3. _____

4. _____

Read Jacob's dream again. Write your interpretation of it in the box below.

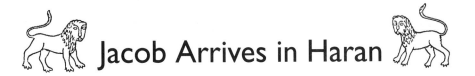

Jacob Arrives in Haran

After he had his dream, Jacob continued on to Haran. At the outskirts of the city, Jacob paused at a well for water. The mouth of the well was stopped up by a rock. People were standing around the well with their sheep, waiting until all the flocks of sheep had been gathered there.

Jacob said to the people, "My friends, where are you from?"

And they said, "We are from Haran."

Jacob asked the people whether they knew his uncle Laban.

And they said, "Yes, we do."

Jacob asked, "Is he well?"

They answered, "Yes, he is. There is his daughter Rachel coming with her father's flock."

He said to them, "Why don't you water your flocks?"

They said, "We cannot until all the flocks have been rounded up. Then the stone will be rolled off the mouth of the well." While he was speaking

with the people, Rachel came with her father's flock. When Jacob saw Rachel, the daughter of his uncle Laban, he went over and rolled the stone off the mouth of the well, and he gave water to the flock of his uncle Laban. Then Jacob kissed Rachel and broke into tears. Jacob told Rachel that he was her father's nephew. She ran and told her father. On hearing the news, Laban rushed to greet Jacob. Laban embraced him and kissed him, and he took him into his house. Jacob told Laban all that had happened, and Laban said to him, "You are truly my bone and flesh."

GENESIS 29:4-14

Jacob Marries

Jacob wanted to marry Rachel. He stayed with his uncle Laban and worked for him. He offered to work for seven years so that he could marry Rachel. Laban agreed.

Meanwhile Laban was planning to play a trick on Jacob. He had another daughter named Leah. Because Leah was older, Laban wanted her to be married first. At the wedding the bride's face was completely covered by a veil. Jacob thought that he had married Rachel.

When morning came, there was Leah.

Jacob said to Laban, "What have you done to me? I worked for you so that I could marry Rachel. Why did you trick me?"

Laban said, "It is not our practice to marry off the younger daughter before the older. Wait until you have been married for one week. Then I will let you marry the other one, too. But you'll have to work for me for seven more years."

And Jacob did so.

GENESIS 29:25-30

Laban's Trick

Laban played a nasty trick on Jacob. Sometimes people cheat others in order to get what they want. Can you think of some other people in the Torah who cheated or deceived others in order to get what they wanted?

Do you think that Jacob deserved to be tricked? Why?

_____

_____

_____

_____

What do you think Jacob learned from the trick that Laban played on him?

_____

_____

_____

_____

Summary

In this chapter you learned about dreams and growing up. You found out that it is possible to interpret dreams. You also read how Jacob the trickster was himself tricked by his uncle. In the next chapter Jacob will encounter his biggest challenge yet—having to face his brother Esau after twenty years.

Jacob Wrestles

It is not easy to say that you are sorry. In Chapter 8 you read how Jacob cheated his brother. In this chapter you will read a Torah text that begins twenty years later, when Jacob returned home and met his brother again. As you read about Jacob's journey home, you will learn about *teshuvah* תְּשׁוּבָה, the changing of one's ways, and *selichah* סְלִיחָה, the seeking of forgiveness.

Jacob Goes Home

After living in Haran for many years, Jacob decided that it was time to return to his home in Canaan. Jacob did not travel alone. A large group went with him, including his two wives, his twelve children, and many servants, friends, and helpers. They traveled with herds of goats, camels, cows, donkeys, and other animals. Help Jacob and his family find their way back to Canaan.

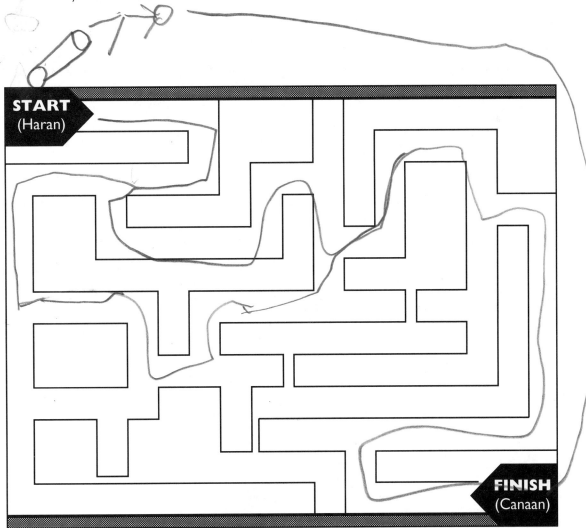

Making Changes: Teshuvah

People often do things that hurt others for which they are sorry afterward. A person who has done a bad deed is not cursed forever to be bad. People can change their bad habits and atone for their wrongs. Judaism provides us with a way to change called *teshuvah*. It consists of four steps.

1. Apologize to the person whom you have wronged, and make sure that your apology is accepted. This step is called *selichah*.

2. Right the wrong that you did. This might mean giving something back or paying to have an item repaired. Sometimes it means accepting some form of punishment.

3. Pray to God for *selichah* and for the strength to avoid doing bad again.

4. Do not repeat the action or deed.

There are times when others may hurt you. Although you do not have to forget the wrong they did, it is a great *mitzvah* to forgive. The Torah teaches that it is wrong to hold a grudge.

Have you ever held a grudge against someone? Has anyone ever held a grudge against you? Write about these times in the space below.

_____

_____

_____

_____

Have you ever asked for *selichah* (forgiveness), or has anyone asked *selichah* from you? Write about these times in the space below.

_____

_____

_____

_____

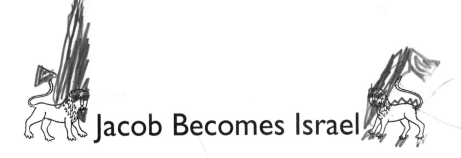

Jacob Becomes Israel

As Jacob neared his old home, he worried about how his brother would react when he saw him. The last time they had seen each other, almost twenty years ago, Esau had said that he was going to kill Jacob. Jacob was afraid that his brother was still holding a grudge against him.

The Torah text that follows tells how Jacob met his brother Esau and how Jacob asked for selichah.

Jacob sent messengers ahead to his brother Esau. He told them, "Speak these words to Esau: 'I stayed with Laban until now. I have cattle, donkeys, sheep, and servants. I send this message to you, my lord, hoping to gain your favor.'"

The messengers returned to Jacob and said, "We went to your brother Esau. He is coming out to meet you, and there are four hundred soldiers with him."

Jacob was very frightened. He divided the people and flocks and herds and camels into two groups. He thought, "This way, if Esau attacks one group, the other may still escape."

That night Jacob arose. Taking his two wives, his two maidservants, and his eleven sons, he went across the Jabbok River. Then he sent across all his possessions.

Jacob was left alone.

A man wrestled with him until morning came. When the man saw that neither of them was winning, he pulled Jacob's hip at its socket so that his hip was strained. Then the man said, "Let me go. The dawn is breaking."

But Jacob answered, "I won't let you go unless you bless me."

The man asked, "What is your name?"

He replied, "My name is Jacob."

The man said, "Your name shall no longer be Jacob. It shall be Israel [God wrestler] because you have wrestled with God and with people, and you have survived."

Jacob asked, "Please tell me your name."

But the man said, "Don't ask my name." And then he left.

Jacob named the place Peniel [Face of God] because "I have seen God face to face. But my life was spared." The sun rose as Jacob, limping on his hip, passed Peniel.

Jacob looked up and saw Esau coming with his four hundred men. Jacob divided the children among Leah, Rachel, and the two maids. He went on ahead and bowed low to the ground seven times until he was near his brother.

Esau ran to meet Jacob. He hugged him and, falling on his neck, kissed him. They cried.

Esau looked around at the women and the children. "Who," he asked, "are these people with you?"

Jacob answered, "God has favored me with many children."

GENESIS 32:4-9, 23-32; 33:1-5

Jacob introduced his family to Esau. They all bowed to show him respect. Then Jacob offered his brother the many gifts that he had brought. The gifts included 200 goats, 200 sheep, 30 camels, and 40 cows. At first Esau did not want to accept them. But Jacob insisted, saying, "Please do me this favor and accept these gifts from me because to see your face is like seeing the face of God. Please accept my presents that I have brought to you. God has treated me well, and I have plenty."

Esau accepted Jacob's gifts, and the two brothers were at peace. They said their good-byes and went their separate ways.

What's in a Name?

In the Torah text that you just read, Jacob was given a new name. From this point on he was known both as Jacob and Israel. This is the first place in the Torah in which we find the word *Israel* יִשְׂרָאֵל. All Jews are descendants of Jacob. At first only Jacob's children were called the Children of Israel or Israelites because their father was called Israel. Later all Jews were called Israelites.

In 1948 a Jewish state was established in the Middle East. Its founders named it Israel for our people and our ancestor Jacob.

Who Wrestled with Jacob?

The big mystery of this Torah text is, Who wrestled with Jacob? In the space below write your opinion about who—or what—wrestled with Jacob that night.

G-d, Because he said I have been watching you and can change your name.

Selichah: Esau and Jacob Are Reunited

The story of Jacob and Esau raises an important question: Did Jacob follow the four steps of *teshuvah* that are listed on page 62? To decide, answer the following questions by checking **Yes** or **No**.

Did Jacob apologize to Esau? ☑ Yes ☐ No

Did Jacob ask for *selichah*? ☑ Yes ☑ No

Did Esau accept Jacob's apology? ☑ Yes ☐ No

Did Jacob right his wrong? ☑ Yes ☐ No

Did Jacob pray and ask for *selichah* from God? ☑ Yes ☐ No

As far as you know, did Jacob repeat any of his wrong actions or deeds? ☐ Yes ☑ No

Do you think that Jacob deserved to be forgiven? ☑ Yes ☐ No

Summary

In this chapter you learned about the four steps of *teshuvah*: asking for *selichah*, righting a wrong, praying, and not repeating a wrong action or deed. You also read the story of how Jacob wrestled and survived and how Jacob's name was changed to Israel. Finally you read about Jacob's reunion with Esau after many years.

In the next chapter you will read about Jacob's children—the Children of Israel—and about Jacob's favorite child, Joseph the dreamer.

Jacob's Children

In Chapter 9 you read that Jacob's name was changed to Israel and that Jacob's children came to be called the Children of Israel or Israelites.

Jacob was the father of thirteen children: Reuben, Simeon, Levi, Judah, Dan, Naphtali, Gad, Asher, Issacher, Zebulun, Dinah, Joseph, and Benjamin. In later years the twelve tribes of Israel were named after Jacob's children. Reuben was the eldest. Benjamin was the youngest. But it was Joseph, the firstborn son of Rachel, who was Jacob's favorite.

▢ ▣ ▢ ▣ ▢ ▣ ▢ ▣ ▢ ▣ ▢ ▣ ▢ ▣ ▢ ▣ ▢ ▣ ▢ ▣ ▢ ▣ ▢ ▣ ▢ ▣ ▢ ▣ ▢ ▣ ▢ ▣ ▢ ▣ ▢

Jacob was settled in the land where his father had lived, the land of Canaan.

When Joseph was seventeen years old, he tended the flocks with his brothers. Joseph often told his father bad things about his brothers. Israel [Jacob] loved Joseph best of all his sons. Joseph was the child of his old age. Israel had a special robe made for Joseph. When the brothers saw that their father loved Joseph more than any of them, they hated him. They did not speak a friendly word to him.

Once Joseph had a dream. He told it to his brothers, and they hated him even more. He said to them, "Listen to this dream that I had. We were tying up bundles of wheat in the field. Suddenly my bundle stood up, and your bundles gathered around and bowed down to my bundle."

His brothers said, "Do you plan to rule over us? Do you plan to control us?" And they hated him even more because of his dream.

Joseph had another dream and told it to his brothers. "In my dream the sun, the moon, and eleven stars were bowing down to me."

When Israel heard about the dream, he said, "What is this dream that you had? Does it mean that your mother, your brothers, and I am to bow down to you?"

GENESIS 37:1-10

Joseph's Two Dreams

In Chapter 8 you read about Jacob's dream of a ladder that reached the sky. You discussed how to interpret Jacob's dream and your own dreams.

The story of Joseph is full of dreams and their interpretations. Try to interpret Joseph's two dreams.

DREAM I

The eleven bundles of wheat are symbols for _The eleven brothers_
_____.

The dream predicts that _Jacob is the ruller_
_of his brothers_____.

DREAM 2

The eleven stars are symbols for _The eleven brothers_.

The sun is a symbol for _Josephes father_.

The moon is a symbol for _Josephes mother_.

The dream predicts that _Josephe is the ruller_
_of his family_____.

Sibling Rivalry

The Torah text tells us how Joseph's brothers felt about him. Joseph and his brothers fought, just as Jacob and Esau did. Brothers and sisters often argue about things. This kind of fighting is called sibling rivalry. *Sibling* means "brother" or "sister." *Rivalry* means "competition."

Imagine that you are the author of the *Torah Times* advice column. Answer the following letter in the space that has been provided.

Dear *Torah Times*:

I have a problem. My brothers hate me because our father favors me the most of all. Why should they be angry at me just because I'm the smartest and most handsome of all my father's sons? I think my older brothers should be proud of me!

Could you give me some advice about how to get along better with my brothers?

Sincerely,
Joseph

Dear Joseph,

Say I am sorry and then them.

Good Luck.
Torah Times

What about Dinah?

The Torah tells us very little about Jacob's daughter, Dinah. One way we can find out about her is by creating our own *midrash*. In order to discover how Dinah felt about Israel's favoring Joseph and about Joseph's dreams, answer the following interview questions in a way that you think Dinah would have.

An Interview with Dinah

Interviewer: Dinah, how does your father's giving only Joseph a special robe make you feel?

Dinah: _aynoer_

_____

Interviewer: Dinah, what do you think of Joseph's dream in which everyone in your family bows down to him?

Dinah: _Ideotic_

_____

Interviewer: Dinah, how do you feel about your brother Joseph?

Dinah: _Selfish_

_____

Interviewer: Dinah, how do you feel about your other brothers' hating Joseph?

Dinah: _good_

_____

Joseph and His Brothers

One day Israel sent Joseph to Shechem to look for his brothers, who were out tending their father's flocks.

The brothers saw Joseph from far off. Before he came close to them, they planned to kill him. They said to one another, "Here comes that dreamer. Come on, let's kill him and throw him into a pit. We can say that a wild animal has eaten him. We shall see what comes of his dreams."

But when Reuben heard this, he tried to save Joseph. He said, "Let's not kill him. Shed no blood. Let's just throw him into the pit out in the desert and leave him." Reuben planned to save Joseph from the others and bring him back to their father.

When Joseph came up to his brothers, they took his robe, the specially decorated robe that he was wearing. They threw Joseph into a pit that was empty, without any water in it.

Then they sat down to a meal. When they looked up, they saw a caravan of Ishmaelites coming. Their camels were taking spice, oil, and perfume to Egypt. Judah said to his brothers, "What do we gain by killing our brother and covering up his blood? Come, let's sell him to the Ishmaelites instead of killing him. After all, he is our brother, our own flesh." Judah's brothers agreed.

The brothers pulled Joseph out of the pit and sold him to the Ishmaelites for twenty pieces of silver. The Ishmaelites then took Joseph to Egypt.

When Reuben returned to the pit and saw that Joseph was gone, he was so upset that he tore his clothes. [Reuben did not know that his brothers had sold Joseph to the traders.] He went back to his brothers and said, "The boy is gone. What am I to do?"

They took Joseph's robe and killed a goat. Then they dipped the robe in the blood. They took the specially decorated robe to their father. He said, "My son's robe. A wild animal has eaten my son." Jacob tore his clothes and cried for his son many days.

Genesis 37:18-34

A Torah Times News Report

Many events occurred in this Torah text. Some readers might have a hard time keeping track of them. You can help.

Imagine that you are a reporter for the *Torah Times*. Complete the details of the news story outlined below.

JOSEPH BELIEVED DEAD

In a tragic turn of events, Joseph, the son of Jacob, _____
_____
_____.

Evidence found at the scene of the tragedy included_____
_____
_____.

Our reporters were able to reach Jacob, the father of Joseph. Although the old man was clearly upset, he told us that_____
_____

_____.

During a recent interview Joseph's eldest brother Reuben said that

_____

_____.

When confronted by our reporters, another brother, Judah, admitted that

_____

_____.

In related news,_____
_____
traders have been seen in the region.

Summary

In this chapter you read the beginning of the story of Joseph the dreamer, the favorite son of Israel. You learned why his brothers came to hate him and how he was sold into slavery. In Chapter 11 you will read how Joseph became a success in Egypt and how he was reunited with his father and brothers.

Joseph in Egypt

In Chapter 10 you read that Joseph was left in a pit by his brothers and taken by Ishmaelite traders to Egypt. In this chapter you will learn how Joseph used his knowledge of dreams to survive in Egypt and to save a people, including his own family, from a terrible famine.

■ ■

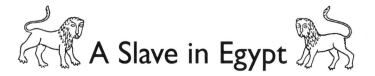

A Slave in Egypt

After Joseph was thrown into a pit by his brothers, they decided to sell him to Ishmaelite traders. Joseph was taken down to Egypt. He was sold to Potiphar, an important official of Pharaoh, the king of Egypt.

God was with Joseph, and he was a successful man. He stayed in the house of his Egyptian master. His master liked Joseph because he saw that God was with Joseph and God made everything that Joseph did successful. He made Joseph his personal attendant and put him in charge of all that he owned.

Joseph was a good-looking man. One day his master's wife cast her eyes upon him and said, "Love me."

But Joseph refused. He said, "My master gives me everything I want and need. I can have anything in this house except you, since you are his wife. How could I do such a wicked thing and sin before God?"

Day after day Potiphar's wife would tease Joseph and try to make him love her. But Joseph wouldn't give in. One day when he came into the house, she grabbed him by his coat and said, "Love me." He broke away, but he left his coat in her hand.

When she saw that she had his coat, she told the servants and then her husband, "The Hebrew slave tried to attack me. When I screamed at the top of my voice, he ran away and left his coat with me."

When Joseph's master heard the story that his wife told him, he was furious. So Joseph's master had him put in prison.

GENESIS 39:1-20

Joseph the Dream Interpreter

In Chapter 10 you learned that Joseph was a dreamer. While Joseph was in prison, he became a dream interpreter. He met two fellow prisoners, a waiter and a baker. One night each man had a strange dream. Joseph explained the meaning of the dreams. Read the two dreams that Joseph interpreted while he was in prison. Try to interpret what the dreams meant.

The Waiter's Dream: In my dream there was a vine in front of me. It had three branches. There were tiny buds on it. Suddenly the buds blossomed and the vine's clusters became grapes. I took Pharaoh's cup, squeezed the grapes into the cup, and gave the cup to Pharaoh.

The Baker's Dream: In my dream there were three baskets on my head. The top basket was full of all kinds of baked food for Pharaoh. And the birds were eating the food out of the top basket.

GENESIS 40:9-11; 16-17

◨ 75 ◧

Write your interpretation of the waiter's dream.	Write your interpretation of the baker's dream.
he is one of pharohs slave	he is pharohs cooker

Below are Joseph's interpretations of the waiter's and the baker's dream. Read Joseph's interpretations and see how he understood the dreams. Compare his explanation of the dreams to your own.

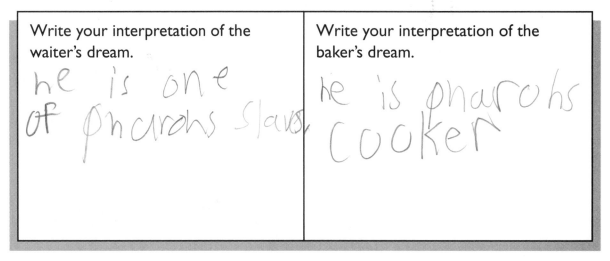

The Waiter's Dream: The three branches are three days. In three days Pharaoh will pardon you and give you back your job. You will serve Pharaoh wine, just as you did before.

GENESIS 40:12-13

The Baker's Dream:

The three baskets are three days. In three days Pharaoh will cut off your head and put it on the end of a pole, and birds will eat your flesh.

GENESIS 40:18-19

Joseph's interpretations of the two dreams came true. In three days the waiter was set free and given back his old job as Pharaoh's waiter. On the same day the baker was put to death.

Pharaoh's Dreams

Two years later Pharaoh dreamed that he was standing by the Nile River. Out of the river rose seven healthy and good-looking cows. They grazed in the reed grass. Then seven more cows came up from the Nile. They were ugly and skinny. They ate up the seven healthy cows. And Pharaoh woke up.

He fell asleep again and dreamed a second dream. Seven healthy ears of grain grew on a single stalk. Behind them sprouted seven dry, thin ears. The seven thin ears swallowed up the seven full ears. Then Pharaoh woke up and realized that it was a dream.

The next morning Pharaoh was upset about his dreams. He sent for all his sages and magicians to interpret the dreams. But none could interpret them for Pharaoh.

Then Pharaoh's waiter remembered the Hebrew youth that he had met in prison. The waiter told Pharaoh about Joseph's ability to interpret dreams.

Pharaoh sent for Joseph, and he was rushed from the prison. After his hair was cut, he changed his clothes and appeared before Pharaoh. Pharaoh told Joseph his dreams.

Joseph said to Pharaoh, "Your two dreams are really the same. God is telling you what is about to happen. The seven healthy cows and seven healthy ears are seven years. The seven skinny cows and the seven dried-out ears are seven years of famine.

"The next seven years will be years of plenty throughout the land of Egypt. After those seven years of plenty will come seven years of famine."

Genesis 41:1-30

A Famine in Canaan

During a famine there is little or no rain. Fields of grain, fruit, and vegetables go dry. Animals die of thirst and starvation. People are sad, hungry, and tired.

Pharaoh appointed Joseph in charge of the entire land of Egypt. During the seven years of plenty, Joseph gathered all the extra grain and stored it. When the seven years of famine came, Joseph opened the storehouses, and the people of Egypt had enough to eat.

The famine had spread all over the world. People from everywhere traveled to Egypt to get food from Joseph.

When Jacob found out that there was food in Egypt, he sent ten of his sons to that country to buy grain. He did not send Joseph's brother Benjamin because he was afraid that something bad might happen to him.

Joseph was the most important official in Egypt. He gave out food to all the people of the land. Joseph's brothers came and bowed low to him, with their faces to the ground. When Joseph saw his brothers, he recognized them. But he pretended that he didn't know them. He asked them harshly, "Where do you come from?"

"From the land of Canaan," they answered. "We came to buy food."

Joseph remembered the dream that he had about his brothers. He said to them, "You are spies. You have come to strip away our land."

They replied, "No. Honestly, we came to buy food. We are twelve brothers, the sons of a man in Canaan. Our youngest brother is now with our father. Another brother is no more."

Joseph said, "Just as I have said: You are spies. Here is how I shall put you to the test. Your youngest brother must come here, or I shall never let you leave this place. Let one of you go and bring back your brother while the rest of you remain imprisoned." He locked them up for three days.

On the third day Joseph said to them, "If you are honest men, let only one of you be held here while the rest of you return home with food for your starving families. But you must bring back your youngest brother to prove that you are honest, so that you will not die."

The brothers said to one another, "We are being punished because of what we did to our brother." Then Reuben spoke up and said, "Didn't I tell you not to hurt the boy? But you didn't listen."

They did not know that Joseph understood what they were saying to one another because the brothers had been using a translator. Joseph turned away from them and cried. When he turned back, he commanded that Simeon be tied up. Then he gave orders to fill the brothers' bags with grain, to return each man's money to his sack, and to give the men food for their journey. The brothers loaded their donkeys and left.

At night they stopped to set up camp. When one of them opened his sack to feed his donkey, he saw the money in his sack. He said to his brothers, "My money has been returned." Their hearts sank. They trembled and turned to one another, saying, "What is this that God has done to us?"

They returned to their father in the land of Canaan and told Jacob all that had happened to them. They said, "The man in charge of the whole country spoke harshly to us. He accused us of being spies and said to us, 'Leave one of your brothers with me. And bring your youngest brother to me so that I shall know that you are honest men. I will then return your brother to you, and you shall be free to move about the land.'"

Jacob said, "Why do these bad things happen to me? First Joseph is no more. Simeon is gone. And now you want to take Benjamin away from me."

Then Judah said, "Father, send the boy in my care and let us be on our way, that we may live and not die. I will guarantee his safety. You may hold me responsible. If I do not bring him back to you, then blame me forever."

GENESIS 42:1-36; 43:8-9

The Second Visit

After much discussion Jacob agreed to let his sons return to Egypt with Benjamin. The brothers took gifts of spice, honey, perfume, pistachios, and almonds with them and twice as much money as they had taken before. They also took Benjamin. They made their way down to Egypt, where they presented themselves to Joseph.

When Joseph saw Benjamin with them, he said to the head of his house, "Fix a big meal. Those men will be dining with me at noon."

The man did as Joseph said. He brought the men into Joseph's house. But they were frightened at being brought there. They thought that it was a trick to attack them and take them as slaves.

"It must be because of the money that was replaced in our bags," they thought. But the head of Joseph's house said, "All is well with you. Do not be afraid." Then he brought Simeon out to them.

When Joseph came home, the brothers gave him the gifts that they had brought. They bowed low before him to the ground.

Joseph greeted them and asked, "How is your father? Is he still in good health?"

They said, "Our father is fine. He is still healthy."

Joseph looked around and saw his brother Benjamin, his mother's other son. He asked, "Is this your youngest brother? May God be good to you, my boy."

With that, Joseph hurried out of the room because he was overcome with feeling. He went to another room and cried. Then he washed his face and came back. Now that he was in control of himself, he gave the order, "Serve the meal."

Then he instructed the head of his house as follows: "Fill the men's bags with food, as much as they can carry. Then put each man's money back into his bag. Put my silver goblet inside the bag of the youngest one, along with his money and food."

Early the next morning the men set out. They had just left the city and had not gone far when Joseph said to his servant, "Go after the men. Ask them how they could repay good with evil. Tell them that they have your master's special goblet."

The servant overtook the men and said, "The one who has the goblet shall be my master's slave. The rest of you shall go free."

Each of the brothers opened his bag. Joseph's servant searched the bags, starting with that of the eldest and ending with that of the youngest. The goblet was found in Benjamin's bag

The brothers returned to the city. They pleaded with Joseph for Benjamin's freedom.

Judah said, "If I return to my father without the boy, my father will die. Because his life is so bound up with the boy's, he will die of grief when he sees that the boy is not with us. I promised my father that I would bring the boy back. Please let me stay as a slave instead of the boy and let the boy go back with his brothers. I cannot return to my father unless the boy is with me. I would not be able to bear my father's misery."

Joseph could no longer control himself in front of his attendants. He cried out, "Have everyone leave me." Only Joseph's brothers were in the room when Joseph made himself known to them. His cries were so loud that the Egyptians could hear them. Joseph said to his brothers, "I am Joseph. How is my father?"

But his brothers couldn't answer him. They were struck dumb by him.

Then Joseph said, "Come forward to me." And when they came forward, he said, "I am your brother Joseph, whom you sold into Egypt. Don't be upset or feel guilty because you sold me here. God sent me here ahead of you to save lives. The famine has been in the land for two years already. There are still five more years before the land will produce anything. It was not you who sent me here but God. God has made me a ruler over the whole land of Egypt."

He went on, "Hurry back to my father. Tell him to come down to me. Tell him that all the family will live near me in Goshen. I will provide you with all that you need. Now hurry and bring my father here."

Then Joseph hugged his youngest brother Benjamin and he cried. And Benjamin also cried. Joseph kissed all his brothers and wept upon them. Only then were his brothers able to talk to him.

GENESIS 43:16 - 45:15

The brothers took their father down to Egypt, and Jacob lived out his life there with all his sons, including Joseph.

Before Jacob died, he blessed each of his sons, as well as the two sons of Joseph, Ephraim and Manasseh. Before Jacob died, he asked that when the Israelites return to Canaan, his sons bury him in the cave of Machpelah, where his grandparents, Abraham and Sarah, were buried, where his parents, Isaac and Rebecca, were buried, and where he had buried his wife Leah. With that, Israel died.

Many years later Joseph died. His last request was that the Israelites take his bones with them when they return to Canaan and bury him with his ancestors.

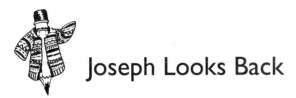

Joseph Looks Back

Imagine that you are Joseph. The story of your life has taken many twists and turns. Review the events of your life by circling the best answers to the following questions.

1. How would you describe your life in Egypt?

    a. It started out well, but it became more difficult as time went on.
    b. My life in Egypt was good, but I missed my family back home in Canaan.
    c. It was wonderful. The Egyptians were very kind.
    d. It was terrible because the Egyptians did not treat Israelites well.

Comment _____

_____

2. Why didn't your brothers recognize you when they came to Egypt?

    a. Many years had passed since I last saw them. I was just a boy when I first came to Egypt.
    b. I had lived in Egypt for so long that I now dressed, spoke, and behaved like an Egyptian.
    c. My brothers had bad eyes and worse memories.

Comment _____

_____

3. Why did you insist on Benjamin's coming to Egypt and then put him through the ordeal of the stolen cup?

    a. I wanted to bring my father to Egypt so that the entire family would be together.
    b. It gave me time to spend with my brother Benjamin.
    c. I wanted to teach my brothers a lesson for selling me.

Comment _____

_____

_____

4. How do you get along with your brothers now?

    a. We are happy to be back together.
    b. My brothers are sorry for what they did to me.
    c. My brothers still do not like me.

Comment _____

_____

5. When you were young, you dreamed that eleven stars, the moon, and the sun were bowing down to you. Has this dream come true for you?

    a. Yes.
    b. No.

Explain _____

_____

6. Do you blame your brothers for selling you into slavery?

    a. Yes. My brothers' hatred made me a slave.
    b. No. I blame my father. If he hadn't made me his favorite, they would not have hated me.
    c. No one is to blame. It was God's will that I be sent to Egypt.

Comment _____

_____

Summary

This chapter completes your study of the Book of Genesis. Genesis began with the birth of the universe and ended with the death of Jacob and Joseph. Genesis has many beginnings and many endings.

In coming chapters you will read Torah texts from the Book of Exodus. You will learn how the Children of Israel became slaves in Egypt and were freed by God. You will read how they wandered in the desert and received the Torah at Mount Sinai.

Genesis Crossword Puzzle

Now that you've completed your study of the Book of Genesis, review all that you've learned by solving this puzzle.

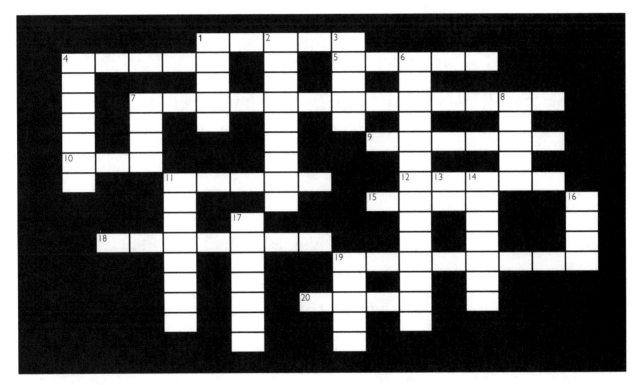

Across
1. Jacob's father-in-law.
4. Story of the binding of Isaac.
5. Abraham's original name.
7. Meaning of *tzedakah*.
9. Rachel to Joseph.
10. Abraham's nephew.
11. Abraham's father.
12. Before you can be forgiven, you must say, "I'm _____."
15. Torah is a Tree of _____.
18. A story that interprets and explains.
19. Forgiveness.
20. Agreement.

Down
1. What Sarah did when she heard that she was going to have a baby.
2. Ceremony of circumcision.
3. Abraham's grandfather.
4. What Noah took into the ark.
6. A *mitzvah* is a Jewish_____.
7. Seventh day: a day of _____.
8. To cut lamb's wool.
11. Righteousness.
13. Eve ate from the Tree ___Knowledge.
14. Isaac's wife.
16. He walked with God and built an ark.
17. Joseph, after his brothers abandoned him, became a _____.
19. Isaac's mother.

CHAPTER TWELVE

A New Generation in Egypt

In this chapter you will begin reading selections from the second book of the Torah, the Book of Exodus. The Hebrew title of this book is Shemot שְׁמוֹת. Like Genesis, Exodus contains stories. Exodus also tells us about many *mitzvot*—Jewish responsibilities or instructions. First you will learn how the Jewish people became slaves in Egypt and you will meet our greatest hero and teacher, Moses. The opening story in Exodus begins many years after Jacob and his family had moved to Egypt.

◻◻◻◻◻◻◻◻◻◻◻◻◻◻◻◻◻◻◻◻◻◻◻◻◻◻◻◻◻◻◻

These are the names of the sons of Israel who went down to Egypt with Jacob. Each one took his family: Reuben, Simeon, Levi, and Judah; Issachar, Zebulun, and Benjamin; Dan, Naphtali, Gad, and Asher.

There were seventy descendants of Jacob, not including Joseph, who was already in Egypt.

Eventually Joseph died, as did all his brothers and that entire generation. The Israelites were fruitful and increased. They multiplied and became many. The land was filled with them.

A new king arose over Egypt who didn't know Joseph. He said to his people, "Look at these Israelites. They are too many. Let us deal cleverly with them so that they don't increase. Otherwise if there is a war, they might join our enemies and fight against us."

So he set masters over the Israelites and forced them into slavery. And the Israelites built the cities Pithom and Raamses for Pharaoh.

But the harder the Israelites were forced to work, the more they increased. The Egyptians feared the Israelites and made them work very hard. They made their lives bitter with harsh labor. They made them use mortar and bricks and do all kinds of work in the field.

And the king of Egypt spoke to the Hebrew midwives, women who helped deliver babies. One of them was named Shiphrah and the other Puah. He said, "When you go to help a Hebrew woman deliver a baby, if it is a boy, kill him. If it is a girl, let her live."

But the midwives feared God and did not do as the king of Egypt had commanded them. They let the Hebrew boys live.

The king of Egypt called for the midwives. He said to them, "Why didn't you do what I ordered? Why did you let the Hebrew boys live?"

The midwives answered Pharaoh, "The Hebrew women are not like the Egyptian women. Because they are quick and active, they have their babies before we can even get to them."

For this reason God treated the midwives well. And the people multiplied and increased in number.

Then Pharaoh ordered all his people, saying, "Every Hebrew boy that is born must be thrown into the Nile River, but every Hebrew girl may live."

EXODUS 1:1-22

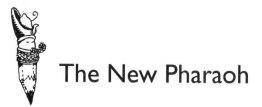

The New Pharaoh

The Torah text says that the new Pharaoh didn't know Joseph. What do you think that this statement means? Look at the choices below. Choose the one that best matches your interpretation.

- [ ] The new Pharaoh hadn't met Joseph.
- [ ] The new Pharaoh had never heard of Joseph.
- [x] The new Pharaoh did not know all the good that Joseph had done for Egypt.
- [ ] The new Pharaoh did not want to know Joseph.
- [ ] The new Pharaoh had forgotten Joseph.
- [ ] The new Pharaoh had forgotten all the good that Joseph had done for Egypt.
- [ ] Other (Write your own reason)

Joseph was dead

During the time of Joseph, Pharaoh and his people liked and appreciated the Israelites. What caused them to change? Why did they begin to fear the Israelites?

There were too many israelites

Pharaoh tried three different ways to control the growth of the Israelites. Go back and find the ways. Then list them below.

1. Slaving them
2. Killing baby boys
3. increased world gloden

Shiphrah and Puah: Heroic Midwives

The two Hebrew midwives Shiphrah and Puah are the heroes of this story. Shiphrah and Puah helped save the Hebrew nation by keeping its male babies alive, even though their actions were against the law.

It would have been easier for Shiphrah and Puah to follow Pharaoh's orders and not risk getting into trouble. Why do you think that Shiphrah and Puah disobeyed Pharaoh's orders? _To save Jewish boys_

The Torah teaches us to follow laws. It also teaches us not to lie. Shiphrah and Puah broke these rules. They lied to Pharaoh and disobeyed his order. But what they did helped save the Jewish people.

Is the Torah teaching us that sometimes we are permitted to break laws or lie? Try to think of a situation when telling a lie or disobeying an order would be the right thing to do. Write about such a situation in the space below.

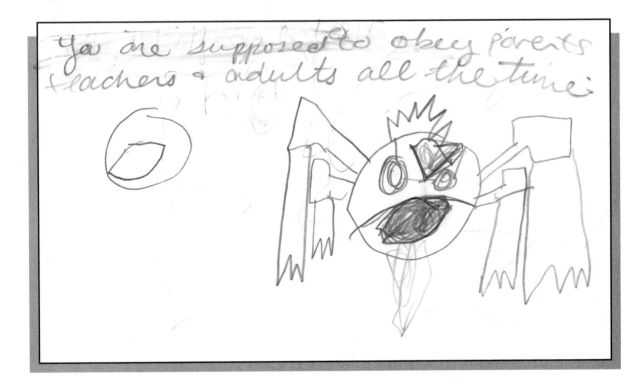

You are supposed to obey parents, teachers & adults all the time.

Moses: A Hero Is Born

*I*n the next Torah text you will read about the birth of a Jewish hero. Moses was born during the terrible time when Pharaoh ordered his people to drown all Hebrew male infants in the Nile River.

A certain man, a descendant of Levi, married a Levite woman. The woman became pregnant and had a son. When she saw how beautiful the baby was, she hid him for three months. When she could no longer hide him, she took a wicker basket and covered it with pitch. She put the child in it and placed it among the reeds by the bank of the Nile River.

The baby's sister stood at a distance to find out what would happen to him.

The daughter of Pharaoh came down to bathe in the Nile. She noticed the basket among the reeds and sent her maid to get it. When Pharaoh's daughter opened the basket, she saw that it contained a child, a boy crying. She felt sorry for him and said, "This must be a Hebrew child."

Then the baby's sister said to Pharaoh's daughter, "Would you like me to get you a Hebrew nurse to feed the child for you?"

Pharaoh's daughter replied, "Yes."

The girl went away and brought back the baby's mother. Pharaoh's daughter said to her, "Take this child and nurse it for me, and I will pay you." So the woman took the child and nursed it.

When the child grew up, the woman brought him to Pharaoh's daughter, and he became her son. She called him Moses because she had drawn him out of the water.

EXODUS 2:1-10

Meet Miriam

The mother of Moses was Yocheved. Her husband was Amram. In addition to Moses, the couple had a son named Aaron. Their daughter was called Miriam. The story tells us a little about Miriam. She watched from a distance when Pharaoh's daughter rescued Moses. She arranged with Pharaoh's daughter to have her mother Yocheved nurse the baby.

Since the Torah doesn't tell us much about young Miriam, you are going to write a *midrash* about her. In the space below write what you think Miriam was thinking as she watched Moses being picked up from the Nile by the maid of Pharaoh's daughter.

MIRIAM'S MIDRASH

As I watched the maid of Pharaoh's daughter pick up my brother, I thought to myself:

Summary dumb mary

You have begun to read from the Book of Exodus. In the opening chapters of Exodus, you learned about the hard life of the Israelites in Egypt. You read how three women—Shiphrah, Puah, and Miriam—performed heroic acts on behalf of the Jewish people and how Moses was saved. In the next chapter you will read how Moses became a great hero.

Moses Learns about Responsibility

In Chapter 12 you read about the birth of Moses. In this chapter you will read about Moses as a young adult. Moses learned to make his own decisions and decided to fight against injustice. As Moses grew and learned to choose between right and wrong, he prepared himself to become a great hero of the Hebrew people.

□ □

A Stranger in a Strange Land

When Moses had grown up, he went out and saw how hard his people were forced to work. He witnessed an Egyptian beating a Hebrew. He looked all around and when he saw that no one was near, he killed the Egyptian and hid him in the sand.

He went out the next day and saw two Hebrews fighting. He said to one of them, "Why are you hitting your fellow?"

The man answered, "Who put you in charge of us? Do you plan to kill me as you killed the Egyptian?"

Moses was frightened and thought, "The deed is known."

When Pharaoh heard about this matter, he wanted to kill Moses. But Moses ran away from Pharaoh. He traveled to the land of Midian and sat down next to a well.

The priest of Midian had seven daughters. They came to draw water and fill their troughs to water their father's flock. But shepherds came and drove them away. Moses stood up and helped them, and he watered their flock.

When they returned to their father, he said, "How is it that you have come back so soon today?"

They answered, "An Egyptian rescued us from the shepherds. He even drew water for us and watered the flock."

He said to his daughters, "Where is he? Why did you leave him? Go find him, and invite him to eat with us."

Moses agreed to live with the man. Moses married the man's daughter Zipporah. They had a son, and Moses named him Gershom because Moses said, "I have been a stranger in a strange land."

EXODUS 2:11-22

From Egypt to Midian

At the beginning of the story, Moses was a prince, living in the palace of Pharaoh. Reread the first paragraph of the Torah text. Put a check next to the emotion that you think best describes Moses at that time.

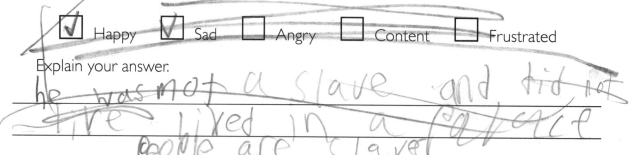

☑ Happy   ☑ Sad   ☐ Angry   ☐ Content   ☐ Frustrated

Explain your answer.

he was not a slave and did not live lived in a palace people are slaves

At the end of the story, Moses is a shepherd. He is living with his father-in-law in the mountains of Midian. Read again the last paragraph of the Torah text. Put a check next to the emotion that you think best describes Moses now.

☑ Happy   ☒ Sad   ☐ Angry   ☐ Content   ☐ Frustrated

Explain your answer.

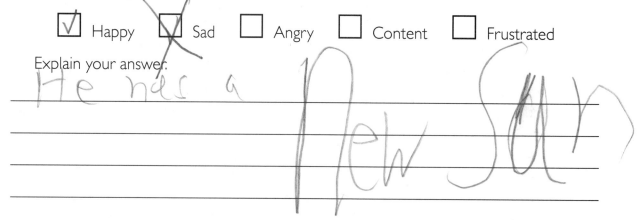

He has a new job

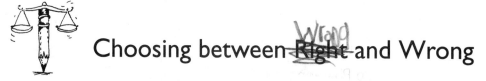

Choosing between ~~Right~~ and Wrong

People have to make decisions every day. Some decisions are more difficult than others. Some are more important than others.

Among the most important decisions that people make are those that deal with ethics. Ethics involves choosing between right and wrong. When people are faced with ethical questions, they sometimes make the wrong choice. It is not always easy to decide between right and wrong.

Almost every hero in the Torah had to face ethical questions. The decisions these people made sometimes changed their lives. Circle what you think is the most important ethical question that each of the Torah heroes listed below had to face. Then tell how the decision each one made changed the person's life.

Abraham had to decide whether to

a. move to Shechem in the land of Canaan.

b. break his father's idols.

c. offer his son Isaac as a sacrifice.

How did this decision change Abraham's life?

B G-Od w us
mersiful

Jacob had to decide whether to

a. bribe Esau for his birthright.

b. help Rebecca at the well.

c. work an extra seven years to marry Rebecca.

How did this decision change Jacob's life?

it changed his relationship with
his brother

Miriam had to decide whether to

a. keep watch over the basket containing her baby brother.

b. offer that her mother help Pharaoh's daughter raise Moses.

c. become a prophet.

How did this decision change Miriam's life?

it allowed her & her mother to
spendmore time with her brother

You read about three ethical decisions that Moses had to make. Use the Torah text to fill in the chart below. Some of the answers have been provided for you.

	What did Moses see?	What was the ethical question that Moses had to answer?	What did Moses decide to do?	Do you think that Moses did the right thing?	How did this decision change Moses' life?
On the first day that Moses went out to see his people . . .		He had to decide whether he should try to stop the Egyptian.			
On the second day that Moses went out to see his people . . .	He saw two Hebrews fighting.				
On the day that Moses went to the well in Midian . . .			He chased away the shepherds.		

Summary

In this chapter you learned about some of the decisions that Moses had to make. These decisions changed Moses' life. In the next chapter you will read how Moses faced the biggest decision of all—whether to return to Egypt and help free the Israelites.

The Burning Bush

In Chapter 13 you read how Moses learned to make ethical decisions. Moses could not stand by while others were suffering. In this chapter Moses was called on to make the most important decision of his life. This time Moses' decision changed the future of the entire Israelite community.

◨ ◨

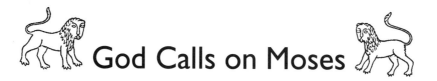

God Calls on Moses

*A*t the end of the last chapter, Moses was living as a shepherd with his father-in-law, Jethro, and his wife, Zipporah. He seemed to have forgotten about the suffering of the Israelites, who were still slaves in Egypt. But God had not forgotten.

Moses kept the flock of his father-in-law, Jethro, the priest of Midian. Moses drove the flock into the desert and came to Horeb, the mountain of God.

An angel of God appeared to Moses in a burning fire coming out of a bush. Moses watched the bush burn and saw that it didn't burn up. Moses said, "I must stop for a moment to look at this marvelous sight. Why doesn't the bush burn up?"

When God saw that Moses had stopped to look, God called to him out of the bush, "Moses. Moses."

And he answered, "Here I am."

And God said, "Do not come any closer. Take off your sandals. The place where you are standing is holy ground. I am the God of your father, the God of Abraham, the God of Isaac, and the God of Jacob."

And Moses hid his face because he was afraid to look at God.

And *Adonai* said, "I have seen the sufferings of My people in Egypt. I have heard their cries. I know their sorrows. I have come down to rescue them from the Egyptians and take them to a good and spacious land, a land flowing with milk and honey, the home of the Canaanites, the Hittites, the Amorites, the Perizzites, the Hivites, and the Jebusites. The cry of the Israelites has reached Me. Come, therefore, I will send you to Pharaoh. You shall free my people, the Israelites, from Egypt."

But Moses said to God, "Who am I? Why should I go to Pharaoh? Why did you choose me to free the Israelites from Egypt?"

God said, "I will be with you. And when you have freed the people from Egypt, you shall worship God at this mountain."

Moses said to God, "When I go to the Israelites and tell them, 'The God of your fathers has sent me to you,' they will ask me, 'What is God's name?' What shall I tell them?"

And God said to Moses, "**Ehyeh-Asher-Ehyeh**, I Will Be Who I Will Be. Thus you shall say to the Israelites, '*Ehyeh* has sent me to you.'"

God said, "Gather together the leaders of Israel and say to them: '*Adonai*, the God of your fathers, the God of Abraham, Isaac, and Jacob, has appeared to me. God said: I will take you out of the misery of Egypt to the land of Canaan, a land flowing with milk and honey.' They will listen to you. Then you shall go to the king of Egypt and say to him: '*Adonai*, the God of the Hebrews, has appeared to us. Please let us go into the desert so that we may sacrifice to our God.' The king of Egypt will not let you go. Of that I am certain. So I will stretch out My hand and strike Egypt with various wonders. Then he shall let you go."

Moses spoke up and said, "But what if they do not believe me and won't listen to me? They will say, `God did not appear to you.'"

Adonai said to him, "What is that in your hand?"

He replied, "A rod."

God said, "Throw it on the ground."

He threw it on the ground, and it became a snake. And Moses was afraid of it.

Then *Adonai* said to Moses, "Reach out your hand and grasp it by the tail."

He reached out his hand and caught it, and it changed back into a rod.

God continued, "Put your hand to your chest."

Moses put his hand to his chest, and when he took it away, his hand was covered with snowy scales.

God said, "Put your hand back to your chest."

Moses put his hand back to his chest, and when he took it away, the skin had turned back to normal.

God said, "If they do not believe either of these two signs and don't listen to you, then take some water from the Nile River and pour it on the dry ground. The water will turn to blood."

But Moses said to God, "O God, I am not a good speaker. I am slow of speech and slow of tongue."

Adonai said to him, "Who gives a person speech? Who makes a person dumb or deaf, seeing or blind? Is it not I, God? I will be with you when you speak. I will tell you what to say."

But Moses said, "Please, *Adonai*, can't you send someone else?"

Adonai became angry with Moses. *Adonai* said, "I know that Aaron the Levite, your brother, speaks well. You and he will meet, and you shall speak to him. You will tell him what to say. He shall speak for you to the people. Take this rod with you so that you can perform the signs."

Moses went back to his father-in-

took the rod of God in his hand.

And *Adonai* said to Moses, "When you return to Egypt, do all the wonders that I have put within your power. But I will harden Pharaoh's heart so that he will not let the people go. Then you shall say to Pharaoh, 'This is what *Adonai* says: Israel is My firstborn child. Let My child go. If you refuse, I will kill your firstborn son.'"

Adonai said to Aaron, "Go into the desert to meet Moses." Aaron went and met Moses at the mountain of God, and he kissed him. Moses told Aaron everything that God had said to him.

law, Jethro, and said to him, "Let me go back to my people in Egypt. I want to see how they are doing."

And Jethro said to Moses, "Go in peace."

So Moses took his wife and sons, mounted them on donkeys, and went back to the land of Egypt. And Moses

Moses and Aaron gathered all the Israelite leaders. Aaron repeated everything that God had said to Moses, and he performed the signs in front of the people. And the people believed Moses and Aaron. The people bowed their heads and worshiped God.

EXODUS 3:1-23; 27-31

Moses the Shepherd

The following *midrash* teaches that God tested Moses before choosing him to lead the Israelites from Egypt. God wanted to make sure that Moses was a *tzadik*.

When Moses was tending the flock of Jethro in the desert, a little lamb ran off to a shady place near a pool of water. Moses ran after the lamb. When he saw it drinking thirstily, he said, "I did not know that you ran away because you were thirsty. You must be weary." And he carried the lamb back to the flock. At that point God said, "Because you showed such mercy with your own flock, you will tend my flock, Israel."

What kind of test would you use to determine if a person is a *tzadik*? Describe your test in the box below.

Watching for God's Wonders

People are often too busy to notice the wonders that God has created. Only when we pay close attention to the world around us can we appreciate its wonders.

After Moses moved to Midian, he learned to pay attention. He watched the goats and sheep as they nibbled on the grass. He stopped to look at the color of the flowers and smell their fragrance. He often said to himself, "God made these things." Moses was paying close attention to his surroundings when he saw the burning bush.

There are many "small" miracles all around you that you probably never noticed. Take a moment now and look around the room. Pay close attention to details. After taking several moments to look around the room, find at least three things that you had never noticed before. Note those things in the box below.

1. _____

_____

_____

2. _____

_____

_____

3. _____

_____

_____

The Reluctant Prophet

Moses was a prophet. A prophet is a person who speaks in God's behalf.

Being God's spokesperson is a hard job. Many people don't want to listen to God. Sometimes a prophet would rather not be a prophet.

Moses was a reluctant prophet. He knew how difficult it would be to speak for God. He knew that Pharaoh didn't want to be told what to do. At first Moses didn't want to be a prophet.

When God asked Moses to speak to Pharaoh, Moses tried to refuse five times. On the next page are the five arguments that Moses gave for *not* going to Pharaoh. Write God's response to each of Moses' arguments.

MOSES' ARGUMENTS	GOD'S RESPONSES
Who am I? Why should I go to Pharaoh? Why did you choose me to free the Israelites from Egypt?	
When I go to the Israelites and tell them, "The God of your fathers has sent me to you," they will ask me, "What is God's name?" What will I tell them?	
But what if they do not believe me and won't listen to me? They will say, "God did not appear to you."	
O God, I am not a good speaker. I am slow of speech and slow of tongue.	
Can't you send someone else?	

Summary

In this chapter you read that God called on Moses to help free the Israelites from slavery in Egypt. You witnessed Moses' struggle to accept his new responsibilities. In the next chapter you will follow Moses as he fights for the freedom of his people and finally leads them out of Egypt.

The Exodus

In Chapter 14 you read about Moses' and Aaron's preparations to challenge Pharaoh to let the Israelites go. In this chapter you will learn how Moses led the Israelites from slavery in Egypt. And you will witness the miracle that took place at the Sea of Reeds.

□ □

Let My People Go!

Having heard the cry of the Israelites, God gave Moses the responsibility of leading the people to freedom. Moses and Aaron set out to try and convince Pharaoh to free the Israelites.

Moses and Aaron went to Pharaoh and said, "So says *Adonai*, the God of Israel: 'Let My people go so that they may celebrate a festival for Me in the desert.'"

But Pharaoh replied, "Who is *Adonai*? Why should I listen and let the Israelites go? I do not know *Adonai*, nor will I let Israel go. Moses and Aaron, why do you distract the people from their tasks? Go back to your work."

That same day Pharaoh instructed the foremen of the people, saying, "Do not give the people any more straw for making bricks. Let them gather straw for themselves. But make them produce the same number of bricks as they have been making until now. Make their work harder and do not let up."

Then Moses returned to God and said, "O *Adonai*, why did You bring harm upon Your people? Why did You send me? Ever since I went to Pharaoh to speak in Your name, he has treated the people worse. You still haven't saved Your people."

Then *Adonai* said, "You shall soon see what I will do to Pharaoh. He shall let them go because of a might stronger than his own. I am God. I appeared to Abraham, Isaac, and Jacob. They called me *El Shaddai*, but I did not make Myself known to them by My name *Adonai*. I also made a covenant with them to give them the land of Canaan.

"I have now heard the crying of the Israelites held in slavery, and I have remembered My covenant. Tell the Israelite people the following: 'I am *Adonai*. I will free you from slavery. I will save you with an outstretched arm and through great punishments. You will be My people, and I will be your God. You shall know that I, *Adonai*, am your God who freed you from slavery. I will take you into the land that I promised to Abraham, Isaac, and Jacob.'"

Adonai said to Moses and Aaron, "When Pharaoh says, 'Show me what your God can do,' tell Aaron to throw his rod down in front of Pharaoh. It will turn into a serpent."

So Moses and Aaron went before Pharaoh and did just as *Adonai* had commanded. Aaron threw down his rod, and it turned into a serpent. Then Pharaoh summoned his magicians, who did the same with their spells. Each one threw down his rod, and the rods turned into serpents. But Aaron's rod swallowed their rods. Still Pharaoh's heart hardened, and he refused to listen to Moses and Aaron, just as *Adonai* had said.

EXODUS 5:1-9, 22-23; 6:1-8; 7:8-13

Does God Have a Name?

In Chapter 13 God was called **Ehyeh-Asher-Ehyeh**, "I Will Be Who I Will Be." The text that you just read contains two other names for God.

God told Moses that the patriarchs knew God as *El Shaddai*, which probably means "God Almighty." This is the name that appears on the outside of a mezuzah מְזוּזָה.

God also said, "My name is יְהֹוָה." No one is sure what this name means. It might mean "God is" or "Infinite God." According to tradition we do not pronounce this name out of respect because it is God's special name. Instead, when we see this name or the abbreviation יְיָ, we say *Adonai*.

Judaism has called God by many names. Some of them include:

Ehyeh-Asher-Ehyeh אֶהְיֶה אֲשֶׁר אֶהְיֶה	"I Will Be Who I Will Be"
Ein Sof אֵין סוֹף	"Endless One"
Ribono shel Olam רִבּוֹנוֹ שֶׁל עוֹלָם	"Ruler of the Universe"
Hakadosh Baruch Hu הַקָּדוֹשׁ בָּרוּךְ הוּא	"The Holy One, Blessed Be"
Ayin Hachayim עֵין הַחַיִּים	"Fountain of Life"

Circle the name that has the most meaning for you. Explain your choice.

_____

_____

_____

_____

The Ten Plagues

Moses tried talking to Pharaoh about letting the Israelites go. That didn't succeed. Pharaoh refused. Then Moses tried working wonders, like turning his rod into a snake. That also didn't succeed. Pharaoh still refused.

Then God caused ten terrible plagues to strike the Egyptians. After each plague Moses asked Pharaoh to let the Israelites go. But each time Pharaoh refused to let the Israelites go free.

The first nine plagues were: (1) The water of the Nile turned to blood; (2) frogs covered the land; (3) lice and vermin infected the Egyptian people and animals; (4) swarms of insects filled the land; (5) disease killed all the livestock of the Egyptians; (6) the Egyptians' skin became inflamed with boils; (7) hail and fire fell on the land of Egypt; (8) locusts ate all the grass and fruit that the hail had left so that nothing green remained; and (9) thick darkness descended upon the land of Egypt. The tenth plague was the most frightening of all.

And *Adonai* said to Moses, "I will bring one more plague upon Pharaoh and Egypt. Then he shall let you go. He will drive every one of you out of here.

"Toward midnight I will go forth among the Egyptians. Every firstborn Egyptian shall die. That includes Pharaoh's firstborn, who sits on his throne, to the firstborn of the slave, who is pushing the millstones, and even the firstborn of the cattle. A loud cry will be heard in all the land of Egypt.

"This month shall be a special time for you. Tell the entire community of Israel that on the tenth of this month, every family shall take a lamb without blemish. And at twilight on the fourteenth day of the month, they shall kill it. They shall put some of the blood on both sides and the top of the doorway of the houses in which they will eat the meat. Then they shall roast the meat and eat it that same night with matzah and bitter herbs.

"Here is how you should eat it: Buckle up, put on your sandals, take your walking stick, and eat it quickly. It is a passover offering to God. I will go throughout Egypt on that night, and I will kill every firstborn Egyptian, both human and beast. The blood on the houses in which you live shall be a

got up in the night, as did all the Egyptians, because there was a loud cry in Egypt. There was not a house that didn't have someone dead. Pharaoh summoned Moses and Aaron in the night and said, "Go, get out of my country. Take the Israelites with you. Go, worship *Adonai* as you said. Take all your animals with you. Get out. Then maybe you will also bring a blessing upon me."

So the people took their dough before it was leavened and wrapped their kneading bowls in their cloaks upon their shoulders. The Israelites journeyed from Raamses to Succoth, about six hundred thousand people, not including children. And they baked matzah with the dough that they had taken out of Egypt.

And Moses said to the people, "Remember that today you went free from Egypt, from the house of slavery. Remember how *Adonai* freed you with a mighty hand."

EXODUS 11:1-6; 12:1-15, 29-39; 13:3

sign. When I see the blood, I will pass over you, so that the plague will not destroy you when I strike the land of Egypt.

"This day shall be a special holiday for you. You shall celebrate it as a festival forever. For seven days you shall eat matzah. On the first day remove all the leaven from your houses. For seven days you shall not eat anything that is leavened."

In the middle of the night, *Adonai* killed all the firstborn Egyptians. Pharaoh

Crossing the Sea of Reeds

When the king of Egypt was told that the Israelites had gone, Pharaoh had a change of heart. He said, "What have we done? Why did we free Israel from slavery?" He called for his chariot and took with him all his soldiers, his six hundred best chariots, and the rest of the Egyptian chariots, with officers in all of them. And *Adonai* hardened Pharaoh's heart, and he chased after the Israelites.

As Pharaoh came near, the Israelites saw the Egyptians catching up with them. They were very frightened and cried out to *Adonai*. They said to Moses, "Did you bring us to die in the desert? Why did you do this to us? Why did you take us out of Egypt? Didn't we say that

we'd rather be slaves in Egypt than die in the desert?"

Moses said to the people, "Don't be afraid. Stand by and watch how God will save you today. For the Egyptians that you see today you will never see again. *Adonai* will do battle for you."

Then Moses held out his arm over the sea, and *Adonai* pushed back the sea with a strong wind and turned the sea into dry ground. The waters split, and the Israelites went into the sea on dry ground. The waters formed a wall for them on their right and on their left. And the Egyptians came into the sea after them.

Then *Adonai* said to Moses, "Hold out your arm over the sea so that the waters may come back over the Egyptians, their chariots, and their horsemen." Moses held out his arm over the sea, and the sea returned to its normal state. The Egyptians tried to run, but *Adonai* threw them into the sea. The waters came back and covered the chariots and horsemen. Of Pharaoh's entire army, not one survived. But the Israelites marched through the sea on dry ground, with the waters forming a wall for them on their right and on their left.

That is how *Adonai* saved Israel that day from the Egyptians. When the people saw *Adonai*'s wondrous power, they feared God. They had faith in *Adonai* and in *Adonai*'s servant Moses.

Then Moses and the Israelites sang this song to *Adonai*. They said,

> I will sing to *Adonai,* the glorious winner.
> *Adonai* has hurled horse and driver into the sea.
> *Adonai* is my strength and my might.
> *Adonai* saves me.
>
> Who is like You, of all the gods?
> Who is like You, majestic in holiness,
> Awesome in splendor, doing wonders?

Then the prophet Miriam, Aaron's sister, took a tambourine in her hand. And all the women went out with tambourines to dance with her. And Miriam sang, "Sing to *Adonai*, the glorious winner. God hurled horse and driver into the sea."

And then Moses brought Israel out of the Sea of Reeds.

<small>EXODUS 14:5-14; 21-23; 26-31;15:1-2,11, 20-22</small>

A Midrash

Our ancestors safely crossed the Sea of Reeds. But the Egyptian soldiers who were chasing them were not so lucky. The Torah tells us that after the last of the Israelites had crossed onto the shore, the sea returned to its normal state, drowning all the Egyptian soldiers.

Should we be happy that our enemies died? The following *midrash* teaches us Judaism's answer.

God does not rejoice at the death of sinners. When the angels saw the destruction of the Egyptians, they wanted to sing. But God silenced them, saying; "That, too, is my own creation, drowning in the sea. And you want to sing songs?"

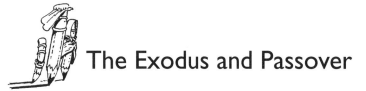

The Exodus and Passover

It is a *mitzvah* to remember the Exodus from Egypt. In the text Moses says, "Remember that today you went free from Egypt."

One of the ways in which we remember the Exodus is by reading from the *haggadah* הַגָּדָה during a Passover seder סֵדֶר. Many parts of the seder can be traced back to this Torah text. Explain the meaning of the following seder symbols.

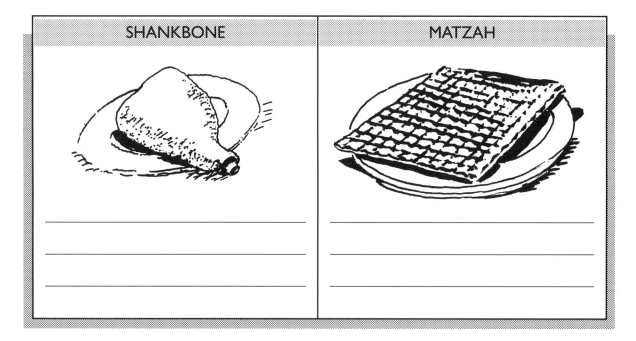

SHANKBONE	MATZAH
_____	_____
_____	_____
_____	_____

MAROR—BITTER HERBS

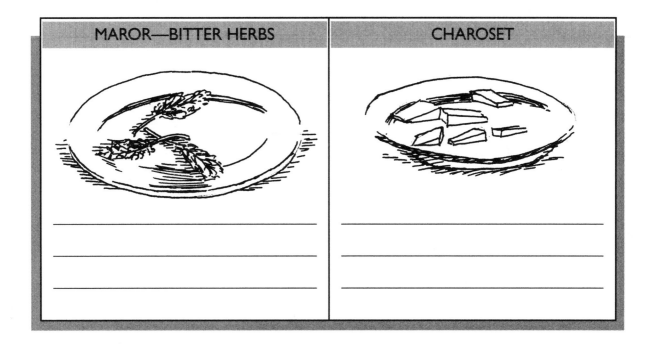

CHAROSET

SALTWATER

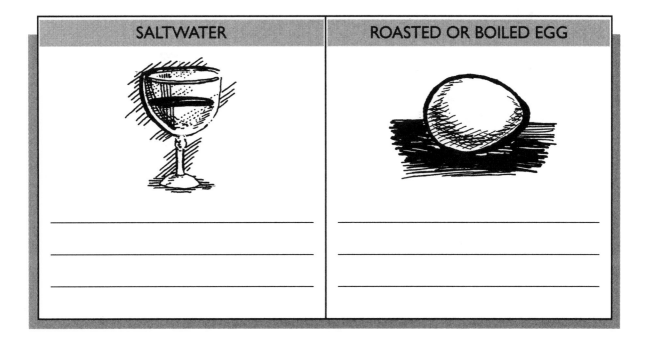

ROASTED OR BOILED EGG

The story of the Exodus from Egypt is a happy one for the Jewish people. But it raises many difficult issues.

Circle one reason why you think the plagues were necessary.

    a. Pharaoh had to be punished.

    b. The Egyptian people had to be punished.

    c. Pharaoh's heart was hardened.

    d. Other

_____

_____

Do you think that the plagues were a fair punishment?

_____

_____

_____

_____

_____

Circle what you think the Torah means when it says that Pharaoh's heart was hardened.

    a. He did not treat the Israelites the same way that he treated his own people.

    b. He became more evil as time went by.

    c. He did not care that people were suffering.

    d. He refused to do *teshuvah* and change his bad ways.

Explain your answer.

_____

_____

_____

_____

Miriam's Dance

After the Israelites were saved at the Sea of Reeds, they showed their appreciation by singing to God.

Then Miriam led a group of women in a dance to God. Why do you think they danced?

_____

_____

_____

List different ways in which people can worship and show their appreciation to God.

_____

_____

_____

_____

Summary

In this chapter you read that Moses and Aaron went to Pharaoh to plead for the release of the Israelites. When Pharaoh refused, God sent a series of plagues on the Egyptians. After the tenth and most horrible plague—the death of every Egyptian firstborn—the Israelites escaped from Egypt by crossing the Sea of Reeds. Once they were free, they celebrated in song.

In the next chapter you will read about a revelation that the entire Israelite nation experienced in the desert. During this event the Israelites were given the Ten Commandments.

The Revelation at Sinai

In Chapter 15 you read that the Israelites were freed from slavery in Egypt. In this chapter you will read about the revelation at Sinai, when God gave the Ten Commandments to the Jewish people. The revelation at Sinai is the great turning point of Jewish history.

□ □

 The Revelation

During a revelation a person "sees" or "hears" God. In most of the revelation stories that you have read, God spoke to only one person. The Torah text you are about to read is different because in it God spoke to the entire nation of Israel and gave the Israelites the Ten Commandments.

The Israelites entered the Sinai Desert during a new moon, exactly three months after they had escaped from Egypt.

And Moses went up to God. *Adonai* called to him from the mountain and said, "This is what you shall tell the Children of Israel: 'You have seen what I did to the Egyptians. You saw how I carried you on eagles' wings and brought you to Me. Now if you follow My instructions and keep My covenant, you shall be a special people to Me. The whole earth is Mine. You shall be to Me a kingdom of priests, a holy nation.'"

God continued, "Tell the people to stay pure. Have them wash their clothes. Let them get ready for the third day. On the third day *Adonai* will come down in the sight of all the people, on Mount Sinai. When the shofar blows a long blast, they may go up the mountain."

Morning came on the third day. There was thunder and lightning, a thick cloud over the mountain, and a very loud blast of the horn. All the people who were in the camp trembled. Moses led the people out of the camp toward God, and they took their places at the foot of the mountain.

Mount Sinai was covered in smoke. *Adonai* had come down upon it in fire. Smoke rose like the smoke from a fireplace. The whole mountain shook violently. The blare of the horn got louder and louder. Moses spoke, and God answered him in thunder.

God spoke all of these words, saying:

"I am *Adonai* your God, who brought you out of the land of Egypt, out of slavery.

You shall have no other gods beside Me. You shall not make statues of anything in the sky, on the land, or in the water. You shall not bow down to them or serve them.

You shall not swear falsely by the name of *Adonai* your God.

Remember the Sabbath and keep it holy. For six days you shall do all your work. But the seventh day is a Sabbath of *Adonai* your God. You shall not do any work. Neither shall your children, your servants, or your animals. For in six days *Adonai* made the heaven and earth and sea and all that is in them. And *Adonai* rested on the seventh day. This is why *Adonai* blessed the Sabbath and made it holy.

Honor your father and mother so that you may last for a long time on the land that *Adonai* your God is giving you.

You shall not murder.

You shall not commit adultery.

You shall not steal.

You shall not tell falsehoods about other people.

You shall not desire the things that belong to other people."

All the people saw and heard the thunder and lightning, the blare of the horn, and the smoking mountain. And when they saw all these things, they fell back and stood at a distance.

EXODUS 19:1-6,10-13,16-19; 20:1-15

 ## At Sinai

A *midrash* teaches that the souls of all Jewish people, not just the people who were alive at the time, were at Sinai during the revelation. God spoke to *all* of us from the mountain.

Because you were also at Sinai, write a firsthand account of what you saw, heard, and felt during the revelation.

MY EXPERIENCE AT SINAI

The Ten Commandments

During the revelation at Sinai, God said ten important things. In Hebrew we call these ten things *Aseret Hadibrot* עֲשֶׂרֶת הַדִּבְּרֹת, which means the "Ten Sayings" or the "Ten Statements." In English we usually call them the Ten Commandments. Let's take a closer look at the Ten Commandments or Ten Sayings.

The First Commandment

I am Adonai יְהֹוָה *your God, who brought you out of the land of Egypt, out of slavery.*

What do you think that the first saying is commanding us to do?

_____

_____

_____

_____

The Second Commandment

You shall have no other gods beside Me. You shall not make statues of anything in the sky, on the land, or in the water. You shall not bow down to them or serve them.

Most Jews today think this saying only prohibits making images that might be used for idol worship. If this commandment only applies to idol worship, do we need to be concerned with it today? After all, who bows down to idols in this day and age?

Actually we do have idols today. An idol doesn't have to be a statue of a god. An idol is anything that people place higher than God. In the space below list any people, places, or things that some might worship as idols.

_____

_____

_____

_____

_____

The Third Commandment

You shall not swear falsely by the name of Adonai your God.

There has been much debate about this saying. Here are some of the ways in which people understand this *mitzvah*. Put a check next to the interpretation that you favor.

 You should not swear or use bad language. Especially don't use expressions that contain the name God or any of God's names.

 You should not make a promise using the expression "I swear to God" (or any other expression that contains the name of God) unless you are sure that you can keep the promise.

 You should not make any promise unless you are sure that you can keep it.

Explain your choice.

_____

_____

_____

The Fourth Commandment

Remember the Sabbath and keep it holy.

Reread the Torah text that explains this commandment. List some of the things that we can do to remember Shabbat and make Shabbat holy.

_____

_____

_____

List some of the things that we should *not* do on Shabbat.

_____

_____

_____

The Fifth Commandment

Honor your father and mother so that you may last for a long time on the land that Adonai *your God is giving you.*

What do you do to honor your parents?

_____

_____

_____

_____

Why is it important to honor your parents?

_____

_____

_____

_____

The Sixth Commandment

You shall not murder.

Place a check [] next to the following statements that you think are correct.

☐ It is murder when a soldier kills during war.

☐ It is murder when a person kills in self-defense.

☐ It is murder when a person kills an animal for food.

☐ It is murder when a person kills an animal for fur or tusks or for display as a trophy.

☐ It is murder when a person kills another person in anger.

☐ It is murder when a person kills an animal that is an endangered species.

☐ It is murder when a person is executed because he or she has committed a capital crime.

The Seventh Commandment

You shall not commit adultery.

The seventh saying is about breaking a special promise. Marriage is a holy *brit*, agreement, or promise between a husband and wife. When people marry, they promise to be faithful to each other. Joseph refused to love Potiphar's wife because he knew that it was wrong to break the covenant between a husband and wife.

List some of the things that husbands and wives can do to keep their marriage holy.

_____

_____

_____

The Eighth Commandment

You shall not steal.

This commandment means that it is wrong to take what is not yours. The Torah teaches us that respect for the property of others is very important. Therefore, we are forbidden from taking anything unless we (1) have paid or traded with the owner for it; (2) have permission from the owner to borrow it; (3) find it and cannot locate the original owner; or (4) receive it as a gift from the owner.

Check those activities in the list below that are prohibited by this commandment.

- ☐ Borrowing a friend's toy without asking permission.
- ☐ Checking out a book from the library.
- ☐ Leaving a restaurant without paying the check.
- ☐ Kidnapping a person.
- ☐ Seizing land on which a family lives and forcing them to leave.
- ☐ Taking candy from a store without paying for it.
- ☐ Keeping a dollar found on the street.
- ☐ Taking medicine from a store without paying for it in order to give it to a poor person who needs it.

The Ninth Commandment

You shall not tell falsehoods about other people.

When you say something untrue about another person, you change the way in which other people think about that person. Long after you have forgotten what you said, others will remember. Think about how people can be hurt by falsehoods. Give an example of a falsehood and the harm that it might cause.

_____

_____

_____

_____

The Tenth Commandment

You shall not desire the things that belong to other people.

The tenth commandment is probably the hardest to observe. Have you ever looked at other people's possessions and wished that they were yours? In the space below write about a time when you desired something that wasn't yours.

_____

_____

_____

_____

 # Types of Mitzvot

There are different ways to classify *mitzvot*. One way is to separate them into positive *mitzvot* and negative *mitzvot*. A positive *mitzvah* is one that tells you to do a certain thing. A negative *mitzvah* is one that tells you *not* to do something. Another way is to classify *mitzvot* according to those that involve action between people and those that are between a person and God.

Complete the chart below by filling in each column. For each *mitzvah*, tell whether it is a positive or a negative *mitzvah* and whether it is a person to person or a person to God *mitzvah*. Then, in the box next to each commandment, number each of the commandments according to how you rate them in importance.

MITZVOT	POSITIVE OR NEGATIVE	PERSON/PERSON OR PERSON/GOD	YOUR RANK
I am *Adonai* your God, who brought you out of the land of Egypt.			
You shall have no other gods beside Me.			
You shall not swear falsely by the name of *Adonai*.			
Remember the Sabbath and keep it holy.			
Honor your father and mother.			
You shall not murder.			
You shall not commit adultery.			
You shall not steal.			
You shall not tell falsehoods about other people.			
You shall not desire the things that belong to other people.			

Summary

In this chapter you read about the most important revelation that the Jewish people experienced. You also learned about some of the meanings of the Ten Commandments.

In the chapters that follow you will read about other *mitzvot* that God gave us. The *mitzvot* found in the Torah instruct us how to do many things, including how to celebrate holidays, how to worship, and how to be holy.

A Temple in the Desert

In Chapter 16 you read about the revelation at Sinai. In this chapter you will read how Moses received instructions from God to build a holy place called the Tent of Meeting. The purpose of this tent was to help the Israelites feel close to God. But the Israelites rebelled. They lost faith in God's presence and began to worship an idol. This act of rebellion threatened to break God's covenant with the Israelites. Moses pleaded with God to forgive the Israelites, and the covenant was saved for future generations.

□ □

Holy Places

Many places are considered holy or special. Your synagogue is a special place where you can pray, learn, and celebrate. Your home is special to you and your family. You might have a special place in your home where your family lights Shabbat candles or where you eat holiday meals. In each of these holy places, you feel special and close to God.

The ancient Israelites also had a place where they felt close to God. While they were wandering in the desert, that holy place was the Tent of Meeting.

Within the Tent of Meeting was another tent or inner room called the *mishkan* מִשְׁכָּן or "dwelling." Within the *mishkan* was a room called the Holy of Holies, a room so sacred that it was only entered once a year by the High Priest. At the center of the Holy of Holies, the Ark of the Covenant, which once contained the tablets of the Ten Sayings, was kept.

God instructed Moses how to build the Tent of Meeting: "Tell the Israelite people to bring Me gifts. You shall accept gifts from anyone who gives from the heart. Have the people make a sanctuary for Me so that I may live among them. I will show you the exact pattern of the *mishkan* and all its furnishings so that you shall make it."

(Exodus 25:1-9)

The Tent and the Temple

The sanctuary described in the Torah was a temporary one. Its walls were made mostly of cloth, like those of a tent. Several hundred years later, King Solomon built the First Temple in Jerusalem. The floor plan of Solomon's Temple was exactly the same as the plan described in this chapter.

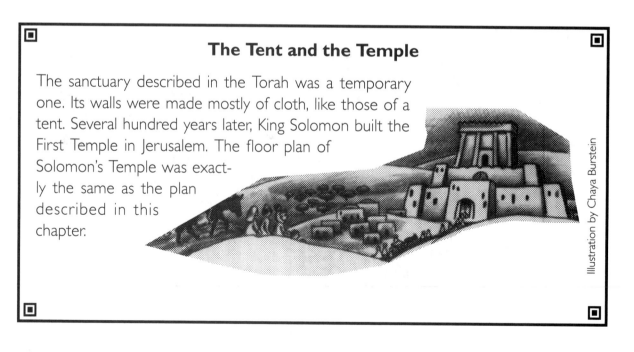

Illustration by Chaya Burstein

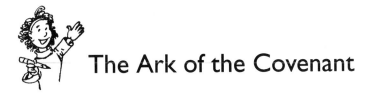

The Ark of the Covenant

The first object that God told Moses to build for the Tent of Meeting was the Ark of the Covenant אֲרוֹן הָעֵדָת. This was a special box or chest that was kept in the Holy of Holies. It was the storage place for the tablets of the Ten Sayings. The ark was made of wood and was overlaid with pure gold.

Your synagogue also has an ark, which is used for storing the Torah. Compare the Ark of the Covenant in Exodus to the ark in your synagogue.

HOW THE ARKS ARE SIMILAR	HOW THE ARKS ARE DIFFERENT
1._____ _____ _____ 2._____ _____ _____	1._____ _____ _____ 2._____ _____ _____

The Menorah

The word *menorah* מְנוֹרָה means "lamp." We usually use this word to refer to the nine-branched candle holder that is used for Chanukah. It is also called a *chanukiah* חֲנֻכִּיָה.

Long before the first Chanukah, the Israelites used the seven-branched menorah in their sanctuary. That menorah was made of solid gold. Today the seven-branched menorah is used in synagogues.

Below are three candle holders. Label each one. Which one is used for Chanukah? Shabbat? The synagogue?

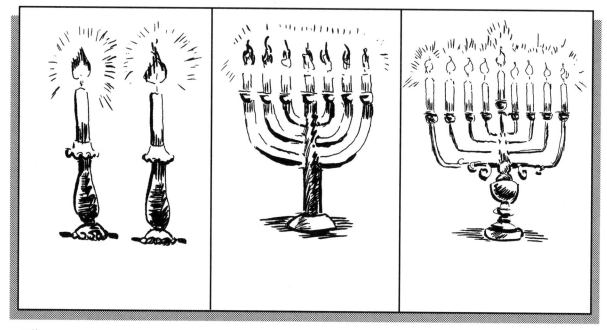

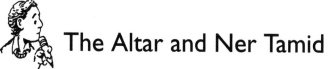

The Altar and Ner Tamid

A special altar was built for burning the various offerings in the Tent of Meeting.

The Israelites were also instructed to place a *Ner Tamid* נֵר תָּמִיד, an "Eternal Light," in the Tent of Meeting. God said to Moses: "Instruct the Israelites to bring you pure olive oil for lighting, to light the *Ner Tamid*. Aaron and his sons shall put them in the sanctuary, outside the curtain over the ark, to burn from evening until morning before God. The light shall be tended by the Israelites throughout the ages." (Exodus 27:20-21)

Where is the *Ner Tamid* in your synagogue?
In the space below make a drawing of the *Ner Tamid* in your synagogue.

Why is the lamp kept burning at all times? What is the *Ner Tamid* a symbol of?

_____

_____

_____

_____

_____

_____

_____

The Role of Priests

Early in Jewish history there were no rabbis. In the Tent of Meeting and in the Temple in Jerusalem, religious duties were performed by priests called *kohanim*. The first priest was Moses' brother Aaron. Aaron's sons and all their descendants were also priests. Today Jewish religious services are usually led by a rabbi.

The Golden Calf

Moses went back up to the mountain, where God gave him the rest of the Torah. Back in the Israelite camp, the people were afraid that God's presence had left them.

When the people saw how long it was taking Moses to come down from the mountain, they gathered against Aaron and said, "Come, make us a god to lead us. We don't know what happened to that man Moses, who brought us out of Egypt."

Aaron said, "Take off the gold rings that are on your ears and bring them to me." And all the people took off the gold rings and brought them to Aaron. He took the rings from the people, melted the gold, and molded it into the shape of a calf.

The people shouted, "This is your god, O Israel, who brought you out of the land of Egypt."

When Aaron saw this, he built an altar in front of the calf. He announced, "Tomorrow shall be a festival of *Adonai.*"

Early the next day the people offered burnt offerings. They sat down to eat and drink. Then they got up to dance.

Adonai said to Moses, "Hurry down. Your people have misbehaved. They have already turned away from the

path that I commanded them. They have made themselves a golden calf and have bowed down to it and sacrificed to it, saying, 'This is your god, O Israel, who brought you out of the land of Egypt.'"

Moses turned and went down from the mountain, holding the two tablets of the Law written in stone. As soon as Moses came near the camp and saw the calf and the dancing, he became very angry. He threw the tablets from his hands and shattered them at the foot of the mountain. He took the calf that they had made and melted it down. He ground it into powder, threw the powder into the water, and made the Israelites drink it.

EXODUS 32:1-6,15,19-20

Aaron and Moses

Why do you think that Aaron listened to the people and made a golden calf?

_____

_____

_____

_____

What do you think Moses would have done if the people had asked him for a god?

_____

_____

_____

_____

How did Moses respond when he returned? Do you think that Moses was right to react the way he did?

_____

_____

_____

A Second Set of Tablets

After the original tablets of the Law were destroyed, Moses asked God to forgive the Israelites for making the golden calf. Moses also asked God to help him lead the Israelites through the desert. God listened to Moses' plea.

God said to Moses, "I will go in the lead and will lighten your burden. . . . I will do as you have asked because you have gained My favor and I have chosen you by name."

Moses said, "Please let me see You."

God answered, "I will let all My goodness pass before you. But you cannot see My face. For no human being may see My face and live. Carve two stone tablets, like the first. I will write on the tablets the same words that were on the first tablets, the ones that you broke."

So Moses carved two stone tablets, like the first. Early the next morning he went up on Mount Sinai with the two stone tablets. *Adonai* came down in a cloud and stood with Moses.

Adonai passed before

Moses and said: *"Adonai, Adonai, a God full of compassion and graciousness; patient, full of kindness and trust, giving kindness to the thousandth generation; forgiving unfairness, lawbreaking, and sin. But God does not pardon all punishment. The bad things that parents do will affect their children and their children's children, to the third and fourth generations."*

So Moses came down from Mount Sinai, holding the two tablets. Moses was not aware that his face was glowing because he had spoken with God.

EXODUS 33:17-34:7, 29

God's Goodness

When Moses asked to see God, God answered, "I will let My goodness pass before you." Then, after Moses had carved a new set of tablets and was about to take them down to the Israelites, God spoke. Beginning with the words "*Adonai Adonai*, a God full of compassion . . .," God listed many of God's characteristics or attributes.

According to some rabbis and scholars, the list contains thirteen different attributes. These include compassion and graciousness, patience, kindness and trust, forgiveness, and justice. We see God through God's attributes.

In the activity below circle the episodes in the Torah in which God's attributes are revealed.

Compassion

a. God appeared to Jacob in a dream of a ladder to heaven.

b. God told Sarah that she would have a son.

c. God caused a flood to wash away all living things.

Kindness

a. God created the world in six days and rested on the seventh.

b. God caused a flood to wash away all living things.

c. God made woman from one side of Adam so that Adam would not be alone.

Forgiveness

a. God gave the Israelites a new set of tablets even though they worshiped the golden calf.

b. God made woman from one side of Adam so that Adam would not be alone.

c. God appeared to Jacob in a dream of a ladder to heaven.

Justice

a. God told Abraham to offer his son Isaac as a sacrifice.

b. God made the snake crawl on its belly.

c. God caused a flood to wash away all living things.

Summary

In this chapter you read that a sanctuary was built in the desert as a place for the Israelites to worship God. But the people turned away from God and worshiped an idol. Although this act almost destroyed the covenant, God showed forgiveness and renewed the covenant for all time.

In Chapter 18 you will read how the ancient Israelites learned to become a holy nation.

CHAPTER EIGHTEEN

You Shall Be Holy

In this chapter you will start to read from the third book of the Torah, the Book of Leviticus. In Hebrew this book is called Vayikra וַיִּקְרָא. Leviticus means "The Levites' Book." The Levites are the descendants of Jacob's son Levi. Leviticus teaches us about many of the things that we can do to be holy.

◻◻◻◻◻◻◻◻◻◻◻◻◻◻◻◻◻◻◻◻◻◻◻◻◻◻◻◻◻◻◻

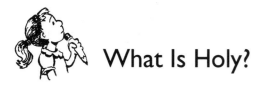 # What Is Holy?

The word *holy* is very difficult to explain. Something that is holy is completely different from anything else. The Hebrew word for *holy* is *kadosh* קָדוֹשׁ. It means "special," "set apart," or "sacred." During a prayer service we recite the words *"Kadosh, kadosh, kadosh is Adonai."*

Think about what makes you feel holy. Complete the sentences below.

I feel holy when _____.

(Describe an activity that is holy for you.)

I feel holy when _____.

(Describe a place that is holy for you.)

I feel holy when _____.

(Describe a time that is holy for you.)

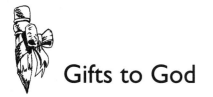 # Gifts to God

We learned in an earlier chapter that people in ancient times believed it was good to give gifts to God. The ancient Israelites offered animals to God as a type of worship and celebration.

The gifts of food brought by the ancient Israelites were called offerings or sacrifices. Offerings were brought at special times and usually involved the whole family. Often the family members would get a share of the food whenever they gave offerings.

Although we don't sacrifice animals to God anymore, we still offer gifts to God. What gifts do we give to God today?

_____

_____

_____

Kosher Food

The Torah teaches us that we should be holy in all aspects of our lives. Judaism not only teaches us how to celebrate and how to worship God. It also guides us how to work, how to play, and even how to eat.

The word kosher כָּשֵׁר *means "fit" or "proper."* Kashrut כַּשְׁרוּת *is the set of rules that tells us which foods may and may not be eaten.* Kashrut *is one way in which the Torah teaches us to bring holiness into our lives. Below are some rules about* kashrut *from the Book of Leviticus.*

Adonai said to Moses and Aaron, "Tell the Israelite people: 'These are the land animals that you may eat. You may eat any animal that has split hoofs and that chews its food. The following animals either don't have split hoofs or don't chew their food, so you can't eat them. They are the camel, the hyrax, the hare, and the pig. The camel, the hyrax, and the hare all chew their food, but they don't have split hoofs. The pig has split hoofs, but it doesn't chew its food.

'Of all that live in the water, whether in the seas or the streams, you may eat anything that has scales and fins. But you must not eat anything in the water that doesn't have both fins and scales.

'The following birds you shall not eat: the eagle, the vulture, the falcon, the raven, the ostrich, the hawk, the sea gull, the owl, the pelican, the stork, the heron, and the bat. You shall not eat all winged insects, except for locusts, crickets, and grasshoppers.'"

LEVITICUS 11:1-23

Is It Kosher?

Refer to the Torah text to find and circle all the animals in the picture below that are considered kosher.

The Holiness Code

So far in this chapter you learned how ancient Israelites made their lives holy by bringing offerings to God and by following the rules of kashrut. Now you will read a Torah text called the Holiness Code. The Holiness Code includes many teachings that show us other ways in which we can live more holy lives.

Adonai said to Moses, "Speak to the whole Israelite community. Tell them:

'You shall be holy, for I, *Adonai* your God, am holy."

Each of you shall respect your mother and father and keep My Sabbath. I am *Adonai* your God.

Do not worship idols or make statues of gods for yourselves. I am *Adonai* your God.

When you harvest your land, do not harvest all the way to the edges of your field. Nor should you go back and pick up fruit that has fallen. You shall leave it for the poor and the stranger. I am *Adonai* your God.

You shall not steal. You shall not lie or trick others. You shall not swear falsely by My name. I am *Adonai*.

You shall not cheat your neighbor. You shall not rob. Pay your workers quickly. You shall not insult a deaf person. Do not put a stumbling block in front of a blind person. You shall be in awe of your God. I am *Adonai*.

You shall not make an unfair decision. Do not favor the poor. You should not prefer the rich, either. Judge your neighbor fairly. Do not gossip. Do not take advantage of any person. I am *Adonai*.

You shall not hate your neighbor in your heart. You may tell your neighbors if they have done something wrong, but do not do anything wrong because of them. Do not seek revenge or hold a grudge against your family. Love your neighbor as yourself. I am *Adonai*.'"

LEVITICUS 19:1-4, 9-18

The Holiness Code and the Ten Commandments

The Holiness Code has often been compared to the Ten Commandments. Below is a list of the Ten Commandments. In the space beside each commandment, write the similar teaching from the Holiness Code. The first one has been done for you.

THE TEN COMMANDMENTS	THE HOLINESS CODE
I am *Adonai* your God, who brought you out of the land of Egypt.	I, *Adonai* your God, am holy.
You shall have no other gods besides Me.	
You shall not swear falsely by the name of *Adonai* your God.	
Remember the Sabbath and keep it holy.	
Honor your father and mother.	
You shall not murder.	
You shall not commit adultery.	
You shall not steal.	
You shall not tell falsehoods about other people.	
You shall not desire the things that belong to other people.	

Read the Holiness Code again. Look for those teachings that are not included in the Ten Commandments. Of those teachings *not* included in the Ten Commandments, write down the one that you found the most surprising.

_____

_____

Which of these teachings do you find the most difficult to understand?

_____

_____

Many of the rules in the Torah were written for people who owned farmland and grew crops. For example: "When you harvest your land, do not harvest all the way to the edges of your field. Nor should you go back and pick up fruit that has fallen. You should leave it for the poor and the stranger." In your own words explain the purpose of this teaching.

_____

_____

_____

_____

How would you follow this teaching today?

_____

_____

_____

Summary

In this chapter you read from the Book of Leviticus, the Torah's guide to holiness. You learned about some of the ways in which people can make their lives holy. In the next chapter you will read about times that are especially holy.

The Israelites Celebrate

In Chapter 18 you read that giving offerings and observing the *mitzvot* of *kashrut* made the Israelites holy. You also read that one of the ways in which holiness is expressed is by how we treat one another. In this chapter you will read a Torah text from the Book of Leviticus that tells how the celebration of certain times of the year helps bring holiness into our lives.

■ ■

Holy Times

There are actions we do to make ourselves feel holy. There are places we can go where we feel holy. And there are special times we set aside when we feel particularly holy.

The following Torah text from Leviticus tells us about six holy times.

Adonai said to Moses, "Tell the Israelites: These are My set times to declare as holy events.

You shall work for six days. But the seventh day shall be a *Shabbat* of complete rest, a holy time.

On the eve of the fourteenth day of the first month, there shall be a *Pesach* offering to *Adonai*. The fifteenth day of the month is *Adonai*'s Feast of Matzah. You shall eat matzah for seven days. Do not work on the first day. It is holy. Do not work on the seventh day. It is holy.

Starting after that first day, bring a sheaf of grain every day as an offering. Count the days for seven weeks plus one day—a total of fifty days. Then you shall bring an offering of new grain to *Adonai*. On that same day you shall hold a celebration. Do not work on that day. It is holy.

On the first day of the seventh month, you shall observe complete rest. It is a holy time, celebrated with loud blasts. You shall not work. You shall bring an offering by fire to *Adonai*.

The tenth day of the seventh month is *Yom Kippur*. It is a holy time for you. It is *Yom Kippur*, on which you atone before *Adonai* your God. It is a *Shabbat* of total rest, during which you shall practice self-denial.

On the fifteenth day of the seventh month, there shall be a Festival of Booths to *Adonai*, lasting seven days. Do not work on the first day. It is holy. For seven days you shall bring offerings to *Adonai*. On the first day you shall bring citrus fruit, palm branches, leafy branches, and willow branches. You shall rejoice before God for seven days. You shall live in booths for seven days so that future generations may know that the Israelite people lived in booths when I brought them out of the land of Egypt. I am *Adonai* your *Adonai*."

In this way Moses declared to the Israelites the set times of *Adonai*.

LEVITICUS 23:1-44

Shabbat: A Holy Day Every Week

The first holy day mentioned in the Torah text is Shabbat שַׁבָּת. We first read about Shabbat in the Creation story. We then read about Shabbat in the Book of Exodus. Observing Shabbat was listed as one of the Ten Commandments.

In the Book of Leviticus, keeping Shabbat was included in the Holiness Code. Shabbat is a holy day that we celebrate every week.

But holy days like Shabbat cannot stay holy without our help. In the space below list some of the things that you can do to help make Shabbat a holy day.

MY PERSONAL SHABBAT

Pesach

Pesach פֶּסַח takes place in the spring, when the weather turns warm after the cold of winter and the flowers begin to blossom. We eat matzah and bitter herbs as we remember the Exodus and how God's wonders freed us from slavery.

People often experience moments when they feel especially free. Sometimes these moments occur after a big change has taken place in their lives or after they have broken old habits.

In the space below write about a time when you felt very free.

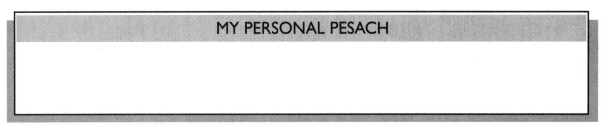

MY PERSONAL PESACH

Shavuot

Shavuot שָׁבוּעוֹת means "Weeks." This holiday takes place early in the summer. To celebrate Shavuot, we count seven weeks plus one day from the beginning of Pesach.

For ancient farmers Shavuot marked the end of the barley harvest that started with Pesach. It was also the beginning of the wheat harvest.

Today Shavuot is the time we celebrate the giving of the Torah at Sinai. On Shavuot we read the section of the Torah that contains the Ten Commandments. Shavuot is a time of finishing and beginning, of counting what we have, and of learning something new.

In the space below write about something new you have learned this year that you can celebrate on Shavuot.

MY PERSONAL SHAVUOT

Rosh Hashanah

Two of the holy days described in this Torah text are known as the High Holy Days. They have become very serious and important days for us. The first of these holy days is Rosh Hashanah רֹאשׁ הַשָּׁנָה, which means "Head of the Year." One of the events that we remember on Rosh Hashanah is the story of Creation. We think of Rosh Hashanah as the birthday of the world.

What gift would you give the world on its birthday?

MY PERSONAL ROSH HASHANAH

Yom Kippur

Ten days after Rosh Hashanah we observe the most solemn of the holy days, Yom Kippur יוֹם כִּפּוּר, the Day of Atonement. The Torah says that on this day we atone before God. To *atone* means to make up for our mistakes. The Torah also tells us that on Yom Kippur we should practice self-denial. *Self-denial* means limiting our desires. It is as if we were telling ourselves, "You can't have that!" Many Jews observe Yom Kippur by fasting. For a full day they do not eat or drink anything.

Think about something that you enjoy but that you could give up for a day. What would you deny yourself as a way of observing Yom Kippur?

MY PERSONAL YOM KIPPUR

Sukot

Sukot סֻכּוֹת takes place in the autumn, five days after Yom Kippur. We celebrate this holiday by bringing food into a booth called a sukah סֻכָּה that we build especially for this festival. We shake two willow branches and three myrtle branches bound together around one palm branch called a *lulav* לוּלָב and a fruit called an *etrog* אֶתְרוֹג.

Originally Sukot celebrated the fruit harvest. Farmers would live in booths in their fields so they could pick all the fruit before the winter frost set in.

During Sukot we remember that God protected us and provided for us in the desert as we made our way toward Canaan. We thank God for life's many blessings. Sometimes our lives are very busy. We forget to thank God for the good things we have.

In the box below list the things for which you are thankful.

MY PERSONAL SUKOT

Did You Know?

When North American pioneers wanted to make a holiday to thank God for bringing them safely to this continent and providing food for their needs, they read the Torah text from Leviticus and modeled their holiday on Sukot. They even set the date of their holiday in the fall, when Sukot is celebrated. That holiday is Thanksgiving!

Which Holy Day Am I?

Below is a game that tests your knowledge of the holy days. Read the description of each holy day. Then write the name of the correct holy day in the proper space.

I am a holy time for you. I occur on the tenth day of the seventh month. I am a day of total rest. You shall practice self-denial on this day. Which holy day am I? _____	I am a festival of freedom. On this holiday God commanded that raised bread should not be eaten. I occur in the spring and remind you that God took you out of Egypt, out of slavery. Which holy day am I? _____
I am the only holy day that is mentioned in the Ten Commandments. I remind people of Creation. Although I am only one day long, I occur more often than any other holy day does. Which holy day am I? _____	I am a day for counting days and sheaves of barley. On this holiday God gave the Torah at Sinai. I occur seven weeks and one day after Pesach. Which holy day am I? _____
I am a holiday of loud blasts. I am a serious day, and I remind people of the birthday of the world. Which holy day am I? _____	On this holiday people "camp out" all week. I am a time during which people say thank you to God for all that they have and eat. On this holiday people shake their branches. Which holy day am I? _____

Summary

In the Torah text from the Book of Leviticus, you read and learned about holiness—holy gifts and foods, holy deeds, and holy days. In the next chapter you will begin reading selections from the next book of the Torah, Numbers, which continues the story of the Israelites as they traveled through the desert.

CHAPTER TWENTY

Counting the People

You will now read from the fourth book of the Torah, Numbers. This book is called Numbers because it begins with a long list, called a census, of the numbers of people in each Israelite family. The Hebrew name for this book is Bemidbar בְּמִדְבַּר, which means "In the Desert." The Book of Numbers continues the story of the Israelites as they traveled through the desert toward the land of Canaan.

▫▫▫▫▫▫▫▫▫▫▫▫▫▫▫▫▫▫▫▫▫▫▫▫▫▫▫▫▫

Scouts in Canaan

*A*s the Israelites prepared to enter the land of Canaan, Adonai *told Moses to send a group of men to scout the land. One man was sent from each of the twelve tribes.*

When Moses sent the men to scout the land of Canaan, he said to them, "Go up to the Negev and the hill country. See what kind of land it is. Are the people who live there strong or weak? Are they few or many? Is the country in which they live good or bad? Are the towns they live in open or walled? Is the soil rich or poor? Is it wooded or not? Be sure to bring back some of the fruit of the land."

They went and scouted the land. When they got to the wadi Eshcol, they cut down a branch with a single cluster of grapes that was so big, it had to be carried by two people. They also took some pomegranates and figs.

After forty days they returned from scouting the land. They went directly to Moses, Aaron, and the whole Israelite community, and they made their report. This is what they said.

"We went to the land that you sent us to. It really does flow with milk and honey. This is its fruit. But its people are powerful, and its cities are huge and protected by walls."

One of the men, Caleb, said, "We should definitely all go up there and take possession of the land. We can do it."

But the other men who had gone with him said, "We cannot attack those people. They are stronger than we are. The men there are giants. We looked like grasshoppers compared to them."

The whole community began to cry. They shouted at Moses and Aaron, "If only we had died in Egypt. If only we might die in the desert. Why did God bring us all this way, just to get us killed in war? We were better off back in Egypt. Let's go back."

But two of the scouts, Joshua ben Nun and Caleb ben Jephunneh, got everyone's attention and said, "The land we crossed and scouted is a very good land. If *Adonai* is pleased with us, then *Adonai* will bring us to that land flowing with milk and honey, and it will be ours. But we must not rebel against *Adonai*."

NUMBERS 13:1-14:9

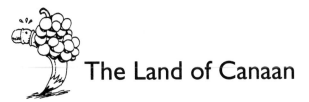

The Land of Canaan

   The Israelites were about to enter a new land. They had many hopes and fears about their life in the land of Canaan. Below are some of the questions that Moses asked the scouts to answer. Provide the reason for each question.

WHAT MOSES ASKED	WHY HE ASKED IT
Are the people who live there strong or weak? Few or many?	
Are the towns open or walled?	
Is the soil rich or poor?	

   Why do you think the Israelites became so upset after they heard the scouts' report?

_____

_____

   How would you have reacted to the scouts' report?

_____

_____

_____

If you were preparing to move to a new country, what are some of the things that you might be afraid of?

_____

_____

What kind of things would you hope to find there?

_____

_____

Help the scouts find grapes in the Promised Land.

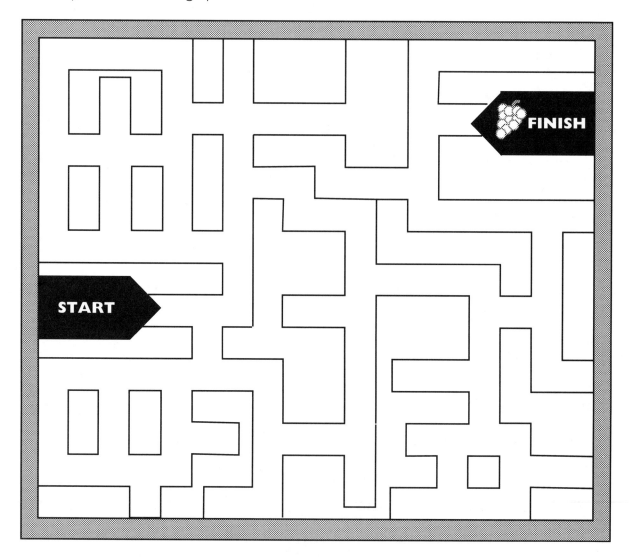

The Corners of Your Garments

The Book of Numbers contains many mitzvot. One mitzvah instructs the Israelites to wear fringes, called tzitzit **צִיצִת**, *on the corners of their garments. The following Torah text tells us about the* tzitzit.

Adonai said to Moses, "Instruct the Israelite people to put fringes on the corners of their garments throughout the ages. They shall attach a fringe with a blue cord at each corner. Tell them: 'That shall be your fringe. Look at it and remember all of God's *mitzvot* and observe them. I am *Adonai* your God, who brought you out of the land of Egypt to be your God. I am *Adonai* your God.'"

NUMBERS 15:37-41

Make Your Own Talit

Today *tzitzit* are attached to a *talit* **טַלִּית**—a special prayer shawl used during synagogue services—or a garment called a *talit katan* **טַלִּית קָטָן**, "little talit," which is worn under a regular shirt.

In the space to the right design or invent your own special garment that reminds you of God's *mitzvot*.

Summary

In this chapter you read from the Book of Numbers about Joshua and the other scouts who were sent to Canaan. You also learned about the *mitzvah* of *tzitzit*. In the next chapter you will read about an evil king who tried to put a curse on the Israelites as they traveled to Canaan.

Bilam and His Donkey

The Torah text in this chapter is an adventure story. It is a story of political intrigue. It is a story of invisible spirits and talking animals. It is the story of a magician named Bilam and an evil king who tried to put a curse on the Israelites.

■ ◨

The Story of Bilam

Before you read the Torah text, you should know something about Bilam. Bilam had a special reputation. People believed that if Bilam blessed them, good things would happen to them. They also thought that if Bilam cursed them, bad things would happen. Because Balak, the king of Moab, wanted to hurt the Israelites, he hired Bilam to curse them.

The nation of Moab was worried because there were so many Israelites. The Moabites were afraid of the Israelites. Balak ben Zippor was king of Moab at that time.

He sent messengers to Bilam ben Beor, saying, "There is a people that came out from Egypt. There are so many of them, they cover the ground. They have moved in next to me. Come and put a curse on them for me. I can't handle them alone. With your curse, maybe I can defeat them and drive them out of the land. I know that whomever you bless is blessed and whomever you curse is cursed."

The Moabite and Midianite leaders went to Bilam with Balak's message. He said to them, "Spend the night here. In the morning I shall give you an answer based on God's instructions."

That night God came to Bilam and said, "What do those people want?"

Bilam said to God, "Balak sent them. He's worried about some people who came out from Egypt. He asked me to curse them before he attacks them so that he can drive them away."

But God said to Bilam, "Do not go with these men. You must not curse that people. They are blessed."

The next morning Bilam told the leaders, "Go home. God will not allow me to go with you."

The Moabite leaders went back to Balak and said, "Bilam refused to come with us." So Balak sent another larger and more important group of leaders to bring Bilam back.

That night God appeared to Bilam and said, "If these men have come to invite you, you may go with them. But you must do whatever I tell you."

The next morning Bilam saddled his donkey and left with the Moabite leaders. But God was unhappy about his going. So God sent an angel to stand in Bilam's way.

The donkey saw the angel of *Adonai* standing in the way, holding a sword in his hand. The donkey swerved from the road and went onto the field. Bilam beat the donkey to make her go back onto the road. Then the angel stood in the middle of the road that passed between two vineyards. There was a wall on both sides. The donkey saw the angel and pressed herself against one side, squeezing Bilam's foot against the wall. So he beat her again.

One more time the angel of *Adonai* moved forward and stood on a spot so narrow that there was no room for the donkey to go to the left or right. When the donkey saw the angel of *Adonai*,

she stopped and lay down, with Bilam still on her. Bilam was so angry that he beat her again with his stick.

Then *Adonai* opened the donkey's mouth and she said, "What did I do to you that you have beaten me three times?"

Bilam said, "You have made a fool of me. If I had a sword, I would kill you right now."

She said, "I am the donkey that you've been riding for a long time. Have I ever done you wrong?" And he answered, "No."

Suddenly *Adonai* opened Bilam's eyes. For the first time he saw the angel of *Adonai* standing in the road with his

sword drawn. Bilam bowed to the ground.

The angel said, "Why have you beaten your donkey? It is I who came out to stop you. When the donkey saw me, she shied away. She saved your life."

Bilam said to the angel of *Adonai*, "It was my mistake. I didn't see you. Do you want me to turn back?"

The angel of *Adonai* answered, "Go with the men. But you may only say what I tell you."

When Balak heard that Bilam was coming, he went out to meet him. Balak said, "When I first invited you, why didn't you come to me? Didn't I offer you enough money?"

Bilam answered, "I am with you now. But I can only say the words that God puts into my mouth."

Bilam followed Balak to a hilltop overlooking the Israelite camp. Bilam prepared to curse the Israelites. But as Bilam began his curse, he could not control the words that came out of his mouth.

Balak brought me from Aram.
The King of Moab brought me from
    the East.
"Come, curse Jacob for me," he said.
"Come, tell of Israel's doom."
How can I curse whom God has not
    cursed?
How can I doom whom God has not
    doomed?

Then Balak said to Bilam, "What have you done to me? I brought you to curse my enemies. Instead, you have blessed them."

Bilam answered, "I can only repeat the words that God puts into my mouth."

Then Balak said, "Come with me. Let's try it again from somewhere else."

They went up to another hilltop called Lookout Point. Bilam approached Balak and his leaders. Bilam began his curse. But *Adonai* put words in his mouth.

Get up, Balak, and listen.
Pay attention, ben Zippor.
No harm is in sight for Jacob.
No trouble in view for Israel.
Their God is with them.
Their Ruler's acclaim is among them.

Balak said, "All right. Do not curse them if you cannot. But do not bless them, either."

Bilam said, "I already told you. Whatever God says I must do."

Then Balak said to Bilam, "Let's try another place. Perhaps God will let you curse them from there." So Balak took Bilam to the peak of Peor.

As Bilam looked out and saw Israel camped, tribe by tribe, the spirit of God came upon him. He began his curse.

How lovely are your tents, 0 Jacob,
Your dwelling places, 0 Israel.

Like palm groves that stretch out,
Like gardens beside a river,
Like aloes planted by God,
Like cedars beside the water.
Blessed are they who bless you.
Cursed are they who curse you.

Balak was furious. He clapped his hands together and said, "I brought you here to curse my enemies. Instead, you have blessed them three times. Go back home. I was going to pay you well. But now God has seen to it that you won't get anything."

Bilam answered, "I was honest from the beginning when your messengers first came. I told them that I could not do anything on my own, good or bad, if it went against God's command."

NUMBERS 22:2-38; 23:6-24:13

An Interview with Bilam

Bilam is a strange character who appears very briefly in the Torah. Let us interview this prophet-for-hire in order to understand him better. Choose the best answer to each question below.

Bilam, why did King Balak of Moab hire you to curse the Israelites?

   a. The Israelites had cursed him first and he was getting back at them.

   b. Balak was jealous of their religion.

   c. He was afraid that they might become a greater nation than Moab was.

At first you did not want to work for Balak. Why not?

   a. God did not want me to curse the Israelites.

   b. I do not like Balak.

   c. Balak did not offer me enough money.

Witnesses say that they saw you beating your donkey. Why did you do that?

   a. The crazy animal kept swerving into a wall.

   b. The donkey was trying to protect me from an angel, but I don't believe in angels.

   c. The donkey began talking to me, and I did not like what she was saying.

What lesson was God trying to teach you by giving your donkey the ability to speak?

a. As we ride the pathways of life, we should stay away from the edges and watch out for angels blocking our path.

b. Just as God gave the donkey the ability to speak, I can only say the words that God puts in my mouth.

c. Never strike a donkey that does not deserve to be hit.

What happened when you finally arrived at Lookout Point and prepared to curse the Israelites?

a. I said good things about Israel, blessing them as God wanted me to.

b. I cursed Balak and the Moabites instead of the Israelites.

c. I made braying sounds, like a donkey trying to speak.

Mah Tovu

Mah Tovu מַה־טֹּבוּ is the first prayer that people sing after they enter the synagogue for morning services. Do you recognize the opening lines of *Mah Tovu*?

Mah tovu ohalecha, Ya'akov,	מַה־טֹּבוּ אֹהָלֶיךָ, יַעֲקֹב,
Mishkenotecha, Yisrael.	מִשְׁכְּנֹתֶיךָ, יִשְׂרָאֵל.
Va'ani berov chasdecha	וַאֲנִי בְּרֹב חַסְדְּךָ
Avo vetecha;	אָבֹא בֵיתֶךָ;
Eshtachaveh el hechal kadshecha	אֶשְׁתַּחֲוֶה אֶל־הֵיכַל קָדְשְׁךָ בְּיִרְאָתֶךָ.
beyiratecha.	

How lovely are your tents, O Jacob,
Your dwelling places, O Israel.
By your abounding love, O God,
I enter Your house;
With awe I worship in Your holy temple.

Bilam's Curse

In the Torah text Bilam agreed to help Balak. But instead of cursing the Israelites, Bilam blessed them three times.

Write a blessing in each of the boxes below. Each blessing should include at least three good things.

BLESSING FOR THE JEWISH PEOPLE

BLESSING FOR _____(Someone You Know)

BLESSING FOR MY FAMILY

Summary

In this chapter you read about Bilam and how he blessed the Israelites, even though he had been hired to curse them. Through God's saving power, King Balak's evil plan was thwarted. In the next chapter you will begin to study the final book of the Torah, Deuteronomy, and you will read about the Israelites' preparations to enter the Promised Land.

Moses Teaches a New Generation

In this chapter you will begin reading several sections from the fifth book of the Torah, Deuteronomy. The word *Deuteronomy* is Greek. It means "Second Torah" or "Retelling of Torah." In this book Moses reviewed the Torah. As Moses prepared for his death, he gave several speeches to the Israelites. Deuteronomy is made up of those speeches. In Hebrew this book is called Devarim דְּבָרִים, which means "Words," because the book begins with "These are the words . . ."

◨ ◧ ◨ ◧ ◨ ◧ ◨ ◧ ◨ ◧ ◨ ◧ ◨ ◧ ◨ ◧ ◨ ◧ ◨ ◧ ◨ ◧ ◨ ◧ ◨ ◧ ◨ ◧ ◨ ◧

Moses Speaks to the Israelites

These are the words that Moses said to all Israel in the land of Moab, on the other side of the Jordan:

"Now, O Israel, pay attention to the laws and rules that I am teaching you, so that you may enter and live in the land that *Adonai,* the God of your ancestors, is giving you."

DEUTERONOMY 1:1, 5; 4:1

Imagine that you are Moses. During the Israelites' forty years of wandering in the desert, many events occurred. You want the people to remember all the events and *mitzvot* of the Torah. In the space below create a poem or song, a list or a mural, a comic strip or a game that reviews the most important Teachings of the Torah.

The Shema

*D*uring his speech to the Israelites, Moses used words that have become the most important prayer of the Jewish religion. That prayer is the Shema שְׁמַע. The word shema means "hear" or "listen." The Shema tells us to listen or pay attention so that we may know that God is One.

What follows the Shema is a prayer called the Ve'ahavta וְאָהַבְתָּ. The word ve'ahavta means "and you shall love." This prayer teaches us some of the ways in which we can show our love for God.

This is the Instruction—the laws and the rules—that *Adonai* your God commanded me to teach you.

Hear, O Israel. *Adonai* is our God, *Adonai* is One.

שְׁמַע יִשְׂרָאֵל, יְיָ אֱלֹהֵינוּ, יְיָ אֶחָד.

And you shall love *Adonai* your God with all your heart and with all your soul and with all your might. Take to heart these words with which I command you this day. Teach them faithfully to your children. Say them when you stay at home and when you are away, when you lie down and when you rise up. Bind them as a sign on your hand. Let them serve as a symbol on your forehead. Write them on the doorposts of your house and on your gates.

DEUTERONOMY 6:1-9

God Is One

The *Shema* says that "God is One." Many people have discussed what this statement means. Check [✔] the opinion below that you agree with the most.

☐ God is the only God.

☐ God is the Number One God.

☐ God is unique.

☐ God is alone.

☐ God is whole and not made of many parts.

☐ God is everything there is.

☐ God is everywhere.

The Ve'ahavta

The *Ve'ahavta* is a list of different ways in which we can express our love for God. The following are two ways in which this Torah text has been interpreted.

The Mezuzah

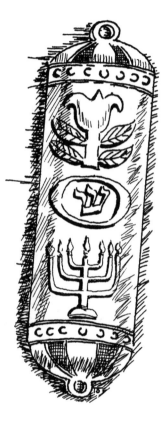

You might recognize the verse "Write them on the doorposts of your house and on your gates." It is the source of the *mitzvah* of putting a mezuzah on our doorposts. *Mezuzah* means "doorpost." We use the word *mezuzah* to describe a box or case that contains a small piece of parchment with the *Shema* and *Ve'ahavta* written on it.

Tefilin

Another *mitzvah* is putting on *tefilin* תְּפִלִּין. These are prayer boxes that are worn by Jews during worship. Putting on *tefilin* is an observance of the instruction "Bind them as a sign on your hand. Let them serve as a symbol on your forehead."

One box is tied around the left arm. The other box is attached to the forehead. Like the mezuzah, both boxes contain parchment with the words of the *Shema* and *Ve'ahavta* prayers.

Interpreting the Ve'ahavta

The *mitzvot* concerning the mezuzah and *tefilin* are based on interpretations of the Torah text. In the space below create two new ways to follow the Torah's instructions based on your own interpretation of the following text: "Bind them as a sign on your hand. Let them serve as a symbol on your forehead. Write them on the doorposts of your house and on your gates."

Summary

In this chapter you read about Moses' speeches to the Israelites. You learned about the origin of the *Shema* and *Ve'ahavta* prayers and studied their meaning. In the next chapter, the last in the Book of Deuteronomy, you will read the final words that Moses said to the Israelite people, as well as the closing words of the Torah.

Moses Says Good-bye

You have reached the final chapter of *Torah: The Growing Gift*. In this chapter you will learn how Moses passed on the leadership of the Israelites to Joshua, who then led the people to the Promised Land. You will also witness the dramatic death of Moses atop Mount Nebo, which overlooks the Promised Land.

□ □

Moses Prepares to Die

M̲oses lived a long and interesting life. According to Egyptian law he should never have been allowed to live. Moses grew up a prince but became a shepherd. He was chosen by God to be a prophet. He defended the weak and fought against the strong. Most important, Moses led the Israelites out of slavery, guided them through the desert for forty years, and taught them God's Torah.

As the Israelites were about to cross the mountains that would lead them into Canaan, the Promised Land, Moses prepared to die. He would never live as a free Jew in a Jewish land.

Moses spoke these words to all Israel: "I am now one hundred and twenty years old. I can no longer be active. *Adonai* has said to me, 'You shall not go across the Jordan.' Joshua is the one who shall lead you."

God said to Moses, "The time is drawing near for you to die. Call Joshua and come to the Tent of Meeting so that I may teach him."

Moses and Joshua went and presented themselves in the Tent of Meeting. God appeared in a pillar of cloud, a pillar of cloud that came to rest at the entrance of the tent.

God said to Joshua ben Nun, "Be strong and steady. You shall bring the Israelites into the land that I promised them."

DEUTERONOMY 31:1-3, 14-15, 23

A New Leader: Joshua ben Nun

Why do you think that Joshua was chosen to be the new leader? What did Joshua do to deserve this honor?

_____

_____

_____

If you were entering a new country and had to choose a new leader, what characteristics would you look for in that leader?

_____

_____

_____

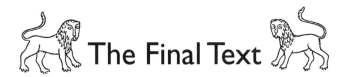

The Final Text

*Y*ou are about to read the final chapter of the Torah. It is a sad ending. But it also marks a new beginning, filled with hope for the people of Israel.

Moses went up from the plains of Moab to Mount Nebo, to a summit facing Jericho. And God showed him the whole land: Gilead as far as the land of Dan; the land of Naphtali; the land of Ephraim and Manasseh; the whole land of Judah, all the way to the Western Sea; the Negev Desert; the valley of Jericho, full of palm trees, all the way to Zoar.

And God said to Moses, "This is the land that I promised to Abraham, Isaac, and Jacob. I am letting you see it with your eyes. But you shall not cross over there."

And so Moses, the servant of God, died in the land of Moab. He was buried by God. No one knows his burial place to this day. Moses was one hundred and twenty years old when he died. His vision was good, and he was still strong. The Israelites mourned for Moses for thirty days.

When the mourning period was over, Joshua ben Nun was filled with the spirit of God because Moses had appointed him. And the Israelites listened to him as God had commanded.

Never again did there rise in Israel another prophet like Moses. God had singled him out, face to face, for the miracles that God had sent him to do in the land of Egypt and for the awesome power that Moses displayed before all Israel.

DEUTERONOMY 34:1-12

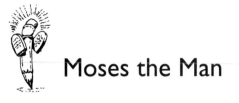

Moses the Man

Moses was a protector and a prophet, a leader and a teacher. List some of the things that Moses accomplished in each of these roles.

MOSES THE PROTECTOR	MOSES THE PROPHET
1._____ _____	1._____ _____
2._____ _____	2._____ _____
3._____ _____	3._____ _____
4._____ _____	4._____ _____

MOSES THE LEADER	MOSES THE TEACHER
1._____ _____	1._____ _____
2._____ _____	2._____ _____
3._____ _____	3._____ _____
4._____ _____	4._____ _____

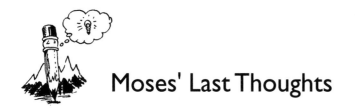

Moses' Last Thoughts

The setting of the last chapter of the Torah is a mountaintop overlooking Canaan. Imagine that you are Moses. Look down from Mount Nebo on the Promised Land. What do you see? How do you feel? What are you sad about? What are you happy about? What are your hopes for the Israelites?

In the box below write a *midrash* from Moses' point of view describing his thoughts and emotions. The *midrash* already has a beginning and an end, taken from the Torah text. Write the middle of the *midrash*.

And God showed him the whole land: Gilead as far as the land of Dan ... all the way to Zoar. And God said to Moses, "This is the land that I promised to Abraham, Isaac, and Jacob. I am letting you see it with your own eyes. But you shall not cross over there."

Moses thought to himself:

And so Moses, the servant of God, died in the land of Moab.

Summary

In this chapter you read the final verses from the Book of Deuteronomy, the last book of the Five Books of Moses. You learned how Moses passed on his leadership of the Israelites to Joshua. Finally you read about the death of Moses, the greatest prophet in Israel. The Book of Deuteronomy marks both the end of an era and the promise of a new beginning in the history of the Jewish people.

Reading the Torah

◧◩◧◩◧◩◧◩◧◩◧◩◧◩◧◩◧◩◧◩◧◩◧◩◧◩◧◩◧◩◧◩◧

Congratulations. You have now completed your study of the Torah.

The Torah is a Tree of Life. It has a beginning and an end. It begins with a birth—the Creation of the world. It ends with a death—the burial of Moses. But it also ends with the seed of a new life—Joshua's leading the people into Canaan.

The rabbis say about Torah: "Turn it and turn it, for everything can be found in it." This means that even as we finish reading the Torah, we can turn it over and begin again to discover new meanings in it.

The Torah is many things. It is a book. It is five books. It is a scroll and a gift and a Tree of Life. Above all, Torah is a Teaching that uses *mitzvot*, stories, and symbols to teach us about ourselves. As you grow older, your understanding of Torah will grow, too. Each year you will learn new ideas and stories. Torah is a growing gift that you will cherish your entire lifetime.